Wonders of the World

A Captivating Guide to Ancient and New Notable Structures

Free Bonus from Captivating History (Available for a Limited time)

Hi History Lovers!

Now you have a chance to join our exclusive history list so you can get your first history ebook for free as well as discounts and a potential to get more history books for free! Simply visit the link below to join.

Captivatinghistory.com/ebook

Also, make sure to follow us on Facebook, Twitter and Youtube by searching for Captivating History.

Table of Contents

Intro

Humans had long been driven by the desire to push the boundaries of what is possible. Alexander the Great, for one, pushed the boundaries of an empire expansion. Claiming the throne at a young age, the Macedonian king dedicated his entire life to uniting different parts of the globe under his rule. From Macedonia to the Greek Peninsula, the young king seized the land of the pharaohs, Persia, and went as far as India, where he faced the fiercest battle he had ever witnessed since claiming the throne. However, his life was not a long one; the Macedonian king died at only thirty-two years old, in 323 BCE.

Ever since the Greeks learned to write, they had been recording every significant event in their realm. They recorded their triumphs over their enemies in a great number of wars, natural disasters that shook the lives of the population, and famines that brought nothing but death to their lands. However, upon Alexander's conquests of much of the western world, these ancient writers were given a way to expand their collection of records. Apart from writing about political shifts in the government and battles between kings, they wrote about structures and buildings.

Following this era of conquests, historians and writers traveled further from the land they called home. The Father of History, Herodotus, for one, is known to have traveled extensively throughout the ancient world to places such as Egypt and Persia. As he crossed one border to the other, he documented his observations and experiences in his renowned work, *The Histories*.

Perhaps intrigued and captivated by the magnificent structures he had encountered throughout his travels, Herodotus thought it would be fitting to record and share them with the world. His writings of these wonders acted as a guide for ancient travelers whose ambition was to tour the globe—just as modern-day tourists use travel guides to visit the most popular points of interest in a certain region. And so, with the help of Callimachus of Cyrene, Herodotus created the earliest list of wonders of the world. Although the list never survived the test of time in its original form, parts of Herodotus' compilation of the wonders of the world were often referenced in other writing sources, therefore giving us a glimpse into a few architectural wonders of the ancient civilizations. Through these passing references, we now have a list of the Seven Wonders of the World.

According to those who referenced Herodotus, the ancient historian had greatly praised the Egyptians, who were considered one of the earliest civilizations to have created such a monumental structure any human could have imagined. Built by the pharaoh Khufu, who reigned over the wealthy kingdom some 4,500 years ago, the Great Pyramid of Giza was designed as a grand tomb, intended to be the final resting place for the Egyptian ruler. Egyptians were the strongest believers of the afterlife; they believed that death was not the end but merely the beginning of another life. The pharaohs themselves were said to have the ability to transform into a god once they passed. So, having a grand tomb was of the utmost importance; this was where his mummy would lay alongside the rest of his items and supplies he might need in the afterlife.

The construction of the Pyramid of Giza no doubt required the combined efforts of thousands of skilled workers and an unwavering dedication to perfection. The structure was expected to have remarkable durability that could not only withstand natural disasters but also the merciless test of time. Towering approximately 138 meters above ground, the Great Pyramid stood as the tallest man-made structure on earth at the time. Built out of 2.3 million stone blocks, each weighing a few tons, the Great Pyramid's construction techniques were indeed unparalleled, even today.

Upon completion, the pyramid boasted a labyrinthine network of passageways and chambers—some said this was to confuse grave robbers. The most prominent section was none other than the King's Chamber, which housed the granite sarcophagus of Pharaoh Khufu. On the outside, the pyramid was covered entirely with a casing of white limestone, which

would gleam under the scorching sun, enticing everyone who passed by the region.

More than a thousand years later, the world was introduced to yet another wonder. The Hanging Gardens of Babylon are believed to be the work of King Nebuchadnezzar II. The gardens stood proudly in the heart of Babylon and served as an enchanting architectural masterpiece to please to king's wife, Queen Amytis, who had been terribly missing the lush greenery of her homeland. (Since the fabled wonder was destroyed completely, leaving us with not even a single piece of ruins, its exact location remains unknown.)

Unlike the rest of the ancient wonders, the existence of these magnificent terraced gardens is disputed among scholars. While those who choose to remain loyal to the ancient writers suggest that the gardens were, in fact, more than just imagination, others claim they were not located in Babylon but in the capital of the Assyrians, Nineveh. Despite the lack of archaeological evidence, ancient writers provided an extensive account of the wonder. Rising above the city, the gardens were an absolute architectural marvel; they were an oasis of lush greenery and vibrant blossoms, providing a clear contrast to the bustling city's surroundings.

The creators of the Hanging Gardens were indeed geniuses. Using colossal stone columns and arches to support the cascading tiers, the gardens appeared as if they were hanging in mid-air. Combined with the fragrance of the flowers in the air and the interplay of light and shadow produced by the sun rays, the Hanging Gardens of Babylon must have been a grand sight.

Travelers of the past were also intrigued by the Temple of Artemis, which could be found at Ephesus (in modern-day Türkiye). The Greeks built this wonder, dedicated to the Greek goddess Artemis, sometime in the 6th century BCE. According to ancient sources, this was the largest temple of the ancient world: measuring at least 137 meters long and surrounded by ornate columns towering over eighteen meters high, the size of the temple doubled even that of the famous Parthenon.

The temple's facade was fully adorned with the exquisite craftsmanship of the ancient Greeks. Apart from intricate sculptures and mythological reliefs, the opulence of the temple was further enhanced by the generous use of gold, marble, and glimmering gems. Within its sanctuary, one could set eyes on the colossal statue of Artemis made entirely out of ebony, gold, and black stone.

Although the Temple of Artemis served as a religious center and was thought to be protected by the gods, an arson took place in 356 BCE, burning the temple to the ground. It was rebuilt following the incident, but an attack by the Goths nearly a century later damaged the temple again. Sadly, it was never rebuilt, and what remains of it today are only remnants of the columns and details recorded by the ancient writers.

In Olympia, Greece, Phidias worked day and night to produce one of his best works yet. The renowned sculptor had been commissioned to create an enormous statue of Zeus, whose grandeur could match the lightning god's celestial powers. Upon its completion sometime in the fifth century BCE, many who set eyes upon it could agree that Phidias had done it again. The seated Zeus was nearly twelve meters tall and lavishly covered in gold and ivory. Its majestic throne, on the other hand, was specially crafted using cedar wood with ivory, ebony, gold, and a few precious stones adorning it. The statue was not alone. Another statue of the winged goddess of victory, Nike, stood on Zeus' outstretched right hand. On his left hand, the lighting god held a piece of scepter with an eagle perched on it.

The colossal statue dwelled within a majestic temple right outside of the Olympia Stadium where the Olympic Games took place. A hexastyle building, the temple was constructed using limestone before being covered with stucco so that it looked like it was constructed from marble. The Doric-style temple also featured thirteen Doric columns on each side and six on each end. Inside were a great number of sculptures carved out of Parian marbles and motifs depicting mythological scenes, including the Twelve Labors of Herakles and the chariot race between Pelops and the son of Ares, Oenomaus. The temple quickly gained the attention of not only religious pilgrims but also various visitors from far and wide who came to Olympia for the Olympic Games.

Meanwhile, Mausolus, the ruler of Caria and the satrap of the Achaemenid Empire, had been planning to build a grand tomb for himself within his capital city of Halicarnassus. The early stages of the construction began in 353 BCE, but Mausolus did not live to see the tomb; he died later that year. The project was never abandoned, as his wife, Artemisia, quickly took the helm and oversaw the construction to completion. Perhaps expressing his love towards her deceased husband, Artemisia spared no expense in seeing the drawing of the tomb brought to life—although she died two years later. She sent messengers beyond her borders to search for the world's best artisans. Word of the construction of such a wonder soon reached Scopas (a renowned sculptor who was in charge of the reconstruction of the Temple of Artemis), and a few other talented artisans, including Leochares and Bryaxis. And so, these men were brought into the city along with a team of hundreds of craftsmen.

The Mausoleum at Halicarnassus was completed in only two to three years. Rising about 45 meters high, it stood on top of a hill overlooking the entire city. The great mausoleum was also designed with meticulous attention to detail, infusing architectural elements originating from Anatolia, Greece, and Egypt. Intricate friezes, sculptural reliefs, stone statues, and scenes depicting the celebrated life of Mausolus were some of the ornamentations found in the tomb.

The great Mausoleum could definitely amaze each passerby in the city; its stepped podium, a colonnade of ornate columns, and the enormous pyramidal roof clearly showed the mixture of influences incorporated into the structure. Most impressive of all, however, was the sculpture crowning the monument. It is believed to have depicted Mausolus and his beloved wife, Artemisia, riding in a chariot drawn by four horses.

The city of Rhodes was also a place where a wondrous monument once resided. The city had just gained victory over the king of Macedon, Demetrius Poliorcetes, who had laid siege to the city for a year. And so, to commemorate their success, the people of Rhodes thought it would be fitting for them to erect a monumental structure to honor their patron god, Helios. The structure is known to us today as the Colossus of Rhodes.

Designed by the renowned sculptor Chares of Lindos, the statue was constructed using bronze and reinforced with iron. Work began sometime in 292 BCE, and its construction spanned over a decade. Once completed, the statue, standing on top of a marble pedestal, impressively towered by the entrance of the city's harbor at approximately twenty-two meters tall—almost the height of New York's Statue of Liberty. Apart from greeting those who arrived at Rhodes by the sea, the Colossus also acted as a guardian of the once-flourishing city.

The most prominent feature of the monument was none other than its delicate sculptures—from the near-realistic features of the face to the stunning musculature of the body. Representing the sun god Helios, the statue wore a crown of pointed sunbeams symbolizing the radiant sun and had a rather triumphant pose with one of his arms outstretched. The statue either held a scepter or had one of his hands shading his eyes just as the depiction of the god found in the city's temple. The Colossus quickly became an iconic symbol of Rhodes, attracting visitors from all over the known world. However, the fate of the wonder was short-lived: an earthquake in 226 BCE destroyed the Colossus, along with many other structures in the city.

In the ancient world, there were no other means of traveling other than by sea. While those entering Rhodes were welcomed by the bronze Colossus, travelers sailing across the Mediterranean would often be left awestruck by the Lighthouse of Alexandria. Also known as the Pharos of Alexandria, the structure was the idea of Ptolemy I, a general who served under Alexander the Great. Given its immense dimensions, the construction of such a structure was indeed an ambitious endeavor. Thus, only the most skillful architects, artisans, and craftsmen were brought into the wealthy city of Alexandria to begin laying the foundation of the grand lighthouse. Among the professionals who designed the wonder was Sostratus of Cnidus, who was also responsible for overseeing the entire execution of the project.

Erected on a small island called Pharos and facing Alexandria, the lighthouse rose to a towering height of about a hundred meters. According to some contemporary writers, the lighthouse was built with two intertwining intentions: to act as a guidance for sailors and as a dedication to the Greek gods Zeus Soter and Proteus, the god of the sea who had the ability to show himself in various forms. Although the Lighthouse of Alexandria was not the first to have been constructed to aid seafarers, it was considered by many as the first monumental one. It eventually earned a spot in the list of the Seven Wonders of the Ancient World and became a symbol of Alexandria's prosperity.

Just like the rest of the wonders of the ancient world, the passage of time was unkind to the Lighthouse of Alexandria. These wonders either succumbed to the merciless wrath of mother nature, warfare, or the changing tides of history. Only the Great Pyramid of Giza stands as the sole survivor. Although considered the oldest wonder of them all, it managed to stand, defying the odds and witnessing all sorts of events and catastrophe caused by the hands of humans or relentless nature.

Indeed, the destruction of these wonders was a loss to human heritage, but their legacy lives on today. The Seven Wonders of the Ancient World gave way for the next generation to broaden their imagination. It is from the remnants of these long-lost wonders that a new set of lists emerged. Known to us today as the Seven Wonders of the New World, each of the structures listed represents a new chapter of human innovation and creativity. Like their ancient counterparts, these wonders were carefully selected to capture the essence of the remarkable advancements of architecture, engineering, and artistry.

The first wonder included in the new list is nestled deep within the rugged sandstone mountains of the present-day Jordan. The city of Petra, known to some as the Rose City, is a particular wonder that possessed a special feature none could ever replicate: instead of being built out of stones, bricks, concrete, and mortars, the city was entirely hand-carved into the rose-colored sandstone cliffs.

The origins of this city can be traced back to the fourth century BCE, and it is said to have been carved by the Nabateans, a nomadic Arab tribe. Begun only as a simple settlement, it did not take long for Petra to grow into an established trading hub completely surrounded by dozens of remarkable buildings. The Al-Khazneh, for instance, is a proof of the Nabateans' engineering prowess. The lack of modern machinery and advanced technology makes this city even more awe-inspiring. Although Petra is located in the middle of a dry desert with nothing but dust, the city is believed to have had its own water management system that could store and channel water to almost every inch of the region.

Despite being a flourishing hub of trade and commerce, Petra was not excluded from tests and obstacles. The once-wealthy city went through a decline and complete abandonment following the shift of trade routes and the rise of bigger and more power-hungry empires.

The title of the second wonder goes to the Great Wall of China, which stretches across the rugged mountains of the Chinese landscape for over 21,000 kilometers. Although considered a wonder of the new world, the Great Wall is rather ancient; the first few parts of the wall were actually built over two thousand years ago, when the Chinese rulers were actively in wars with each other and a few foreign powers. Beginning from a series of independent walls constructed by different states of ancient China, the structure evolved into a unified wall under the kingdom's first emperor, Qin Shi Huang.

Of course, with such a monumental structure, the construction was not at all an easy walk in the park; its construction process is considered the dark side of the wonder. Historians have estimated that the construction involved at least a few million workers ranging from different classes of Chinese society—from soldiers to peasants and prisoners. These people were mostly forced laborers who toiled for years, no matter the weather and conditions, to realize their emperor's vision of a fortified border.

Constructed using a variety of architectural techniques and materials, such as tamped earth, wood, and stone, the wall indeed prevented several invasions and attacks laid by those who dwelled beyond the Chinese frontiers. However, apart from its military significance, the Great Wall also possesses a great cultural and symbolic importance for the Chinese people of the ancient and modern world. While the wall was once built to hold off foreigners, today, the Great Wall openly welcomes people from all over the world.

The Romans also successfully immortalized their influences. In the heart of their ancient capital, Rome, stands a grand amphitheater called the Colosseum. Back then, the majestic structure was known as the Flavian Amphitheater. Commissioned by the emperor Vespasian as a gift to his subjects, the Colosseum was also aimed to showcase the might of the powerful Roman Empire. It served as a center of entertainment for the Roman citizens. In the amphitheater, citizens were presented with extravagant spectacles, such as theatrical performances, animal hunts, mock battles, and most popular of all, gladiatorial games.

Today, the Colosseum does not appear to be in its best condition. However, back when it was in its glory, the elliptical structure's immense size included a circumference of almost 175 meters. It rose over four stories high, with a total of eighty-eight arches of the same size. As the largest amphitheater in the empire, the Colosseum was made to hold an estimated 50,000 to 80,000 spectators across its tiered seats. Its travertine stone façade would entice every visitor to stop by and marvel at its grandeur, while the complex underground system and passages, though barely visible to the spectators, have completely enthralled historians and archaeologists alike.

The Colosseum was the empire's precious symbol of imperial power. Its construction was a testament to Rome's vast wealth. Sadly, when the empire declined, so did the Colosseum. After surviving earthquakes, fires, and even looting, the structure was neglected following the Sack of Rome.

On the other side of the globe, specifically within the heartland of the Yucatan Peninsula, the world was introduced to another wonder that never fails to capture the interest of modern historians and explorers. Known as the Chichen Itza, this archaeological site transports its curious visitors to a time when the Mayan civilization was at its peak. The city was

constructed sometime around the fifth century CE. However, despite the discovery of many artefacts and ruins once belonging to the lost civilization, Chichen Itza is still shrouded in mystery.

The ancient Mayan city was once invaded by the Spanish conquistadors and left forgotten for centuries. It was then rediscovered by two explorers who had ventured onto the peninsula in search of any traces left by the Mayans. While some claim that the site of Chichen Itza was a common knowledge to the locals, others agree that the rediscovery brought it to the world stage, where it began receiving much-deserved attention.

Beginning as a modest settlement, Chichen Itza evolved into a major urban center over the centuries; it was not only a hub of religious activity but also a political and economic center. As the melting pot of cultural exchange, Chichen Itza had a diverse set of architectural pieces, each featuring amalgamations of different cultures, including those of the Toltecs and the Olmecs. The Temple of Kukulkan (El Castillo) is the epitome of Maya-Toltec artistry.

While the Mayans were known for Chichen Itza, the Inca civilization was renowned for its very own city, Machu Picchu. Meaning "Old Mountain" in the Quechua language, it is no surprise that the city is located high amid the Andes Mountains of Peru, hidden from the outside world. After its abandonment following the Spanish invasion, the once majestic city was left untouched until it was reclaimed by mother nature. Machu Picchu was brought back to life—as an archaeological site and tourist destination rather than a bustling city-when it was accidentally discovered by the American explorer Hiram Bingham.

Following the discovery, a few of Machu Picchu's secrets began to unfold, but many still await to be deciphered. The city may give us insights into the lives of the Inca, but scholars still debate the main purpose of the city. Whether it was strictly used for religious purposes or simply a residential getaway for the nobles, none can exactly confirm. Nevertheless, its mysterious air and impressive architecture continuously welcome countless visitors who wish to embark on a journey through time.

Meanwhile, those who prefer to listen to the story of love beyond measure might get intrigued by the next wonder: the Taj Mahal. Standing on the banks of India's Yamuna River, the grand mausoleum is considered a symbol of eternal love and architectural brilliance. It was commissioned by the Mughal emperor Shah Jahan as his last gift to his beloved wife, Mumtaz Mahal, who passed away during childbirth.

The most magnificent feature of the Taj Mahal is its symmetrical proportions, which can be seen in every section of the mausoleum—except the tomb chamber of Mumtaz Mahal. While the mausoleum itself is the complex's centerpiece, the Taj Mahal is also accompanied by lush, manicured gardens and a reflecting pool that enhances the wonder's ethereal beauty. The dome itself looks as if it nearly touches the heavens, with the glistening finial providing an extra touch to the structure.

The Taj Mahal's facade is covered in white marble, causing the mausoleum to slightly change colors depending on the time of day. Both the interior and exterior are adorned with intricate motifs and calligraphic inscriptions of the Quran. Unlike a few other wonders of the new world, the Taj Mahal never experienced a period of neglect. To this day, its allure has inspired not only historians and artists but also romantics and writers.

The last wonder of the new list lies on top of the Corcovado Mountain in Rio de Janeiro, Brazil. This colossal statue is said to have been built as a symbol of faith. Popularly known as Christ the Redeemer, the iconic statue was inaugurated in 1931, making it the youngest of the New Seven Wonders. Specially designed by the Brazilian engineer Heitor da Silva Costa, the statue towers over the city at approximately thirty-eight meters above ground.

Constructed out of reinforced concrete and covered in soapstone, the giant statue exudes a soft glow whenever it is hit by the Brazilian sunlight. The statue's facial features have been perfectly sculpted into an expression full of compassion and serenity. With its arms outstretched, the statue of Christ the Redeemer welcomes its visitors with an all-encompassing love.

These wonders, both ancient and new world alike, hold a profound significance that goes beyond their physical features. These architectural splendors are not just relics of the past. They are the proofs of human achievements that have shaped the world we have come to know today. And so, preserving these sites is more than crucial: these wonders allow us to connect with our history and learn an array of lessons from the past. The Pyramids of Giza and the rest of the ancient world wonders provide us with passage to the past, offering glimpses of the lives that thrived before us. The new wonders, such as Petra, Machu Picchu, and the Taj Mahal demonstrate how humans can push their creative boundaries and evolve through different periods and regions.

Indeed, preserving the wonders is not a responsibility that should be carried by only one individual. These sites belong to all of humanity; thus, their conservation is a collective endeavor. But of course, keeping these sites intact is easier said than done; several significant challenges need to be taken into account. Natural disasters, climate change, tourism pressures, and urbanization can all pose an obstacle to the effort.

Nevertheless, the importance of preserving these wonders cannot be overstated. These sites are not only a testament to our shared history and cultural heritage but also serve as sources of inspiration, education, and pride. By preserving these wonders, we ensure that future generations can continue to marvel at their beauty and significance. We provide an opportunity for people from all walks of life to connect with their roots, to understand the complexities of our world, and to appreciate the rich tapestry of human civilization.

Part 1: Seven Wonders of the Ancient World

A Captivating Guide to the Great Pyramid of Giza, Hanging Gardens of Babylon, Temple of Artemis, Statue of Zeus, Mausoleum at Halicarnassus, and More

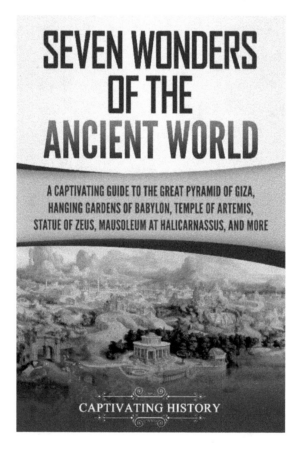

Introduction

The Seven Wonders of the Ancient World are widely considered to be a testament to the ingenuity and technological advancements of ancient civilizations. Despite the fact that many of these structures no longer exist today, they continue to capture the imagination of people around the world. According to historical research, the Seven Wonders of the Ancient World were heavily influenced by Hellenistic culture and were chosen based on their grandeur and sophistication.

The Seven Wonders of the Ancient World are as follows:

- The Great Pyramid of Giza
- The Hanging Gardens of Babylon
- The Temple of Artemis
- The Statue of Zeus
- The Mausoleum of Halicarnassus
- The Colossus of Rhodes
- The Lighthouse of Alexandria

Of these, only the Great Pyramid of Giza still exists today.

Herodotus, a historian who lived from circa 484 to 425 BCE, was one of the earliest writers to document the Seven Wonders of the Ancient World. However, it is important to note that his writings may not be entirely accurate. Luckily, we don't have to take just his word for it, as other authors, such as Strabo, Diodorus, and Philo, also wrote about the ancient wonders.

According to archaeologists Peter Clayton and Martin Price, the lists of the Seven Wonders of the Ancient World were more deeply ingrained during the Renaissance period. However, it is important to note these lists were primarily based on Greek perspectives since Greek authors constituted the vast majority of writers during that era. Consequently, several regions, such as Asia, Africa, and the Americas, were excluded from the lists created in the past.

One of the Seven Wonders of the Ancient World that has been the subject of much debate is the Hanging Gardens of Babylon. Despite the fact that Herodotus, also known as the "Father of History," does not mention the Hanging Gardens of Babylon, other authors, such as Strabo and Philo, claim the gardens existed and were destroyed in an earthquake during the 1st century CE.

What happened to the other wonders? Well, the Statue of Zeus slowly fell into ruin after the Olympic Games were banned once Christianity took root. Christians saw the games as a pagan rite. As a result, Olympia, where the Statue of Zeus was located, fell into disuse. The statue was eventually taken to Constantinople, where it was destroyed in an earthquake around the 5th or 6th century CE.

The Temple of Artemis was destroyed by a mob led by Saint John Chrysostom in 401 CE, becoming yet another victim of the spread of Christianity. The Mausoleum of Halicarnassus was also affected by the religion, as it was dismantled and used by the Knights of Saint John of Rhodes (also known as the Knights Hospitaller) for their castle in Bodrum after the structure was destroyed by a series of earthquakes.

The Colossus of Rhodes was built by the Rhodians for three hundred talents and stood for fifty-six years before being destroyed. It was eventually sold to a Jewish merchant from Edessa in 654 CE. Finally, the Lighthouse of Alexandria was destroyed in 1480 after a series of earthquakes. Today, the Citadel of Qaitbay stands in its place.

But what did the Seven Wonders of the Ancient World mean to the people who saw them? This book will pull back the curtain to explore why these structures were so significant. As you explore the information in this book, you will likely come to realize why the Seven Wonders of the Ancient World still intrigue and inspire us today. After all, it is hard not to be inspired by the idea that something as great as a 455-foot-tall pyramid could happen when diverse skills and capabilities are pooled together.

Summary of events:

- c. 2550 BCE: Pharaoh Khufu (Cheops) initiated the construction of the Great Pyramid of Giza.
- c. 605–562 BCE: Legends suggest that King Nebuchadnezzar II built the Hanging Gardens of Babylon.
- c. 550 BCE: The reconstruction of the Temple of Artemis began in Ephesus.
- c. 456 BCE: The construction of the Temple of Zeus was finished.
- c. 435 BCE: Phidias created the Statue of Zeus in the Temple of Zeus at Olympia.
- c. 356 BCE: An intentional fire destroyed the Temple of Artemis at Ephesus.
- c. 323 BCE: The restoration of the Temple of Artemis occurred.
- c. 353–350 BCE: The Mausoleum of Halicarnassus, the burial place of King Mausolus of Caria, was built.
- c. 300–246 BCE: The Lighthouse of Alexandria was constructed.
- c. 292–280 BCE: The Colossus of Rhodes, a statue of Helios, stood in the harbor of Rhodes.
- c. 228 or 226 BCE: An earthquake caused the collapse of the Colossus of Rhodes.
- 262 CE: The Goths pillaged and demolished the Temple of Artemis at Ephesus.
- 395 CE: The Statue of Zeus was relocated to Constantinople.
- 401 CE: A Christian mob possibly destroyed the Temple of Artemis at Ephesus.
- 475 CE: According to Byzantine historian Zonaras, the Statue of Zeus was destroyed in a fire in Constantinople.
- c. 654 CE: Theophanes, a Byzantine historian, claimed that a Jewish merchant transported the fallen Colossus of Rhodes to Edessa to be melted down.
- 956 CE: An earthquake caused the partial collapse of the Lighthouse of Alexandria, which had previously been damaged in 950 CE.

- c. 1100 CE: After repairs, a domed mosque was added to the Lighthouse of Alexandria.

- c. 1330 CE: The Lighthouse of Alexandria ultimately collapsed due to an earthquake.

- c. 1494 CE: Portions of the Mausoleum of Halicarnassus were repurposed as walls in the Castle of Saint Peter at Bodrum by the Knights of Saint John of Rhodes.

Chapter 1 - The Great Pyramid of Giza

In the fascinating annals of Egypt's history, before the appearance of the Great Pyramid of Giza, two pivotal events stand out as profound landmarks in the evolution of pyramid construction. These events, separated by centuries, left an indelible mark on Egypt's architectural landscape and exemplify the remarkable ingenuity and vision of the ancient Egyptians.

The first of these monumental events took place during the 27th century BCE, a time when a chancellor named Imhotep lived. Imhotep was renowned for his multifaceted talents as an architect, high-ranking official, and polymath, and he graced the stage of history with an awe-inspiring creation: the Saqqara Step Pyramid.

Rising majestically in the lands of Saqqara, Egypt, this architectural marvel holds the distinction of being the first pyramid constructed in Egypt. Imhotep, driven by an unyielding desire to honor Pharaoh Djoser, embarked on an audacious endeavor to fashion a monumental structure that would transcend the boundaries of tradition.

Imhotep's brilliance shone through as he harnessed his architectural genius to fashion an unprecedented royal burial complex. The Saqqara Step Pyramid stands as a testament to Imhotep's visionary design and unwavering commitment to architectural innovation.

The architectural grandeur of the Saqqara Step Pyramid is a sight to behold. It is composed of six mastabas, rectangular structures with gently sloping sides, seamlessly stacked upon one another. Soaring to a height of approximately 205 feet (62 meters), this awe-inspiring creation was an unprecedented achievement of its time.

Centuries later, the chronicles of pyramid construction in Egypt took another momentous turn with Pharaoh Sneferu, who commissioned Egypt's first true pyramid, known as the Red Pyramid.

Nestled amidst the landscape of Dahshur, Egypt, the Red Pyramid stands as a testament to Sneferu's determination to surpass the architectural achievements of his predecessors. Its elegant and refined form with smooth, sloping sides heralded a transition from the previous step pyramid design. The Red Pyramid represents a significant milestone, an architectural turning point that would forever shape the legacy of pyramid construction in ancient Egypt. Clad in a resplendent coat of red limestone, which gave it its name, this remarkable edifice has withstood the relentless march of time, despite the removal of its original casing stones.

These two extraordinary landmarks—the Saqqara Step Pyramid and the Red Pyramid—served as the harbingers of a new era in the realm of monumental architecture in ancient Egypt. They laid the foundation for the subsequent construction of the iconic pyramids at Giza, leaving a mark on the sands of time.

Introduction to the Great Pyramid of Giza

The pyramids of Giza, which were erected during the Fourth Dynasty, stand proudly on the banks of the Nile River in northern Egypt. These magnificent structures were constructed by pharaohs who sought to honor the gods and ensure a prosperous afterlife by filling the tombs with opulent treasures. Dating back to the Old Kingdom, approximately 4,500 years ago, these remarkable constructions were built under the rule of Khufu, Khafre, and Menkaure.

Let's delve into the basic yet intriguing details of each pyramid:

1. Pharaoh Khufu: The Great Pyramid was erected around 2550 BCE. This colossal structure was meticulously assembled using a staggering 2.3 million carved stone blocks. Soaring to an initial height of 481.4 feet (146.6 meters), it reigns supreme as the largest pyramid in Egypt, captivating all who behold its grandeur.

2. Pharaoh Khafre: Nestled amidst the Giza Plateau, the pyramid belonging to Khufu's son, Khafre, is a majestic sight. Constructed between 2558 and 2532 BCE, it stands shoulder to shoulder with

the enigmatic Great Sphinx, a fascinating amalgamation of a lion's body and a pharaoh's noble countenance. This pyramid, measuring 471 feet (143.5 meters) in height, takes its place as the second-largest pyramid in Egypt.

3. Pharaoh Menkaure: Continuing the lineage of pyramid construction, Menkaure, the son of Khafre, crafted a smaller yet intricately designed pyramid sometime between 2532 and 2503 BCE. Although it is the smallest among the trio, with an original base measuring approximately 356 feet (108.5 meters) on each side and a height of about 215 feet (65.5 meters), its elegance and attention to detail make it an architectural gem in its own right.

It is important to note that the precise measurements of these pyramids vary slightly depending on the source, and there is always the potential for new discoveries that might shed more light on how tall the pyramids once were. The pyramids' heights have diminished over the centuries due to the removal of their outer casing stones, which were used for other construction projects.

The pyramids of Giza stand behind the smaller pyramids that are known as the Queen's Pyramids. From left to right: the Pyramid of Menkaure, the Pyramid of Khafre, and the Great Pyramid of Khufu.

The Pyramid of Khufu

The Great Pyramid, also known as the Pyramid of Khufu, stands as an awe-inspiring architectural marvel in Giza, Egypt. Historical records indicate this monumental structure was completed during the reign of Khufu, the second pharaoh of the Fourth Dynasty of the Old Kingdom of Egypt. Originally towering over 481 feet (146.6 meters) in height, its current height stands at approximately 455 feet (around 139 meters) due to the loss of its exterior stone casing. Upon its completion, the Great Pyramid proudly claimed the title of the tallest structure in the world, maintaining this distinction until the construction of England's Lincoln Cathedral in 1311.

The Great Pyramid's remarkable alignment, with each side displaying an angle of approximately 51.5 degrees, stands out as one of its most notable features. This architectural masterpiece was constructed using a combination of limestone and granite, with the core composed of limestone and the exterior adorned with granite. The process of building the pyramid involved the movement and placement of over two million individual rocks.

In 2016, Egyptologist Mark Lehner and engineer Glen Dash conducted a groundbreaking study to validate a long-standing theory suggesting that the pyramid possessed a slightly lopsided appearance, with the eastern side being shorter than the western side. Employing cutting-edge technologies like laser scanning and 3D modeling, they attempted to measure the pyramid's original height. The outcome of their research uncovered fascinating insights into the vertical dimensions of the pyramid's sides. According to the study's findings, the eastern face displayed a remarkable range in original height, spanning from an impressive 755.561 to 755.817 feet (equivalent to 230.295 to 230.373 meters). The western façade fluctuated between 755.833 and 756.024 feet (approximately 230.378 and 230.436 meters). These results show that a mere 5.55 inches (or 14.1 centimeters) separated the two.

Upon entering the Great Pyramid, one would discover a total of seven boat pits distributed strategically throughout its chambers. Two pits lie on the south side, two on the east side, two are situated between the Queen's Pyramids, and one rests adjacent to the funerary temple and causeway. One of the most fascinating findings within the pyramid was the discovery of a remarkably well-preserved boat crafted from hardwood planks. Measuring around 142 feet in length, the boat's purpose and usage remain shrouded in mystery. It is likely the ship would have symbolized the barge that the sun god Ra uses to cross the sky.

Nestled southeast of the Great Pyramid are three smaller pyramids, two of which were dedicated to the wives of Khufu, namely Queen Henutsen and Queen Meritites. Another pyramid was erected in honor of Khufu's mother, Queen Hetepheres.

The Great Pyramid has three chambers. The King's Chamber is a red granite room accessed through a vast gallery. This chamber houses an empty royal sarcophagus. To safeguard the King's Chamber, an ancient mechanism was positioned in front of it, designed to deter potential burglars by lowering massive blocks in their path. Despite these protective measures, the chamber was ultimately subjected to theft.

An entrance measuring fifty-nine feet grants access to the northern part of the pyramid. The entrance leads to a downward-sloping corridor connecting to an unfinished underground room. Situated at the heart of the pyramid lies the Queen's Chamber, which is accessible through the descending corridor and linked to the burial chamber, also known as the King's Chamber.

The purpose of the Queen's Chamber has long been a topic of debate among Egyptologists. While the traditional belief suggests that the chamber was intended for the burial of a queen, recent research has cast doubt on this assumption. The chamber's design closely resembles the subterranean chamber beneath the pyramid, yet its true purpose remains uncertain.

The air shafts in the King's and Queen's Chambers have also been a subject of contention among researchers. Egyptian archaeologist Zahi Hawass states that the air shafts in the Queen's Chamber extend quite far but eventually reach a dead end. Conversely, Egyptologist Miroslav Verner argues that the air shafts in the King's Chamber lead outside the pyramid, proposing that they might even lead to Khufu's actual burial chamber since his sarcophagus was empty when it was explored in the late 18th century. Hawass further notes that the Great Pyramid stands apart from the other pyramids in Egypt due to its door featuring copper handles, igniting speculation about potential concealed secrets.

Recent research has employed muon imaging. Muons are high-energy particles that continually descend upon Earth, and they are used to probe the internal structure of the Great Pyramid of Giza. By utilizing this method, researchers have identified a sizable void situated above the pyramid's Grand Gallery, a lengthy corridor linking the King's Chamber and the Queen's Chamber. This void spans approximately ninety-eight feet in length and twenty feet in height. The research also unveiled evidence of a smaller secondary void beyond the pyramid's northern face.

It is vital to acknowledge that this research is in its preliminary stages, necessitating further investigation to unveil the precise nature and purpose of these voids. The discovery of these enigmatic spaces has ignited immense interest and triggered spirited debates among scholars, but their exact purpose and contents continue to elude us.

It is commonly acknowledged that the construction of the Pyramid of Khufu demanded an immense amount of time and labor. Estimates suggest that over 230 cubic meters of stone were laid daily throughout Khufu's approximate thirty-year reign (he ruled anywhere from twenty-three years to sixty-three years).

The social status of the workers involved in building the Great Pyramid remains a subject of debate among scholars. It was once commonly accepted that the pyramids were built using slave labor. However, many historians argue against the notion that these workers were slaves, citing the Diary of Merer as evidence to support their claim. This ancient Egyptian logbook provides detailed accounts of the transportation of limestone from Tura to Giza during the pyramid's construction. The logbook depicts a well-organized workforce led by a supervisor who was responsible for efficiently transporting materials across significant distances.

However, it is important to note that the logbook does not offer direct evidence of this crew's involvement in constructing the Great Pyramid specifically. Nevertheless, the information within the logbook suggests the workers who dedicated themselves to building the pyramids were not slaves but highly skilled laborers.

Recent studies on the construction of the Great Pyramid of Giza have shed light on the diverse materials used to create it. These materials include limestone sourced from the Tura quarry in Egypt and cedarwood imported from Lebanon. The successful transportation of these materials across vast distances stands as a testament to the logistical and organizational capabilities of the ancient Egyptians.

The Pyramid of Khufu is the largest of the three main pyramids at Giza.

The Pyramid of Khafre

The Great Pyramid of Giza is the pyramid that is listed as one of the Seven Wonders of the Ancient World. However, it is worth delving into the background of the other pyramids at Giza since they are all awe-inspiring. When Khufu, the father of Khafre, passed away, Khafre did not immediately succeed him. Instead, Khafre's older brother, Djedefre, ascended the throne and constructed his own pyramid at Abu Rawash, located about five miles north of Giza. Sadly, the passage of time has left the pyramid mostly in ruins.

Djedefre ruled Egypt for approximately ten to fourteen years before his demise, leading to Khafre assuming the throne. Khafre returned to Giza and set out to erect his pyramid, which originally towered at a height of 471 feet. Today, it stands at around 448 feet. Though slightly smaller in size than the Pyramid of Khufu, the Pyramid of Khafre appears taller due to its elevated location and the use of unique construction materials.

Unlike the Pyramid of Khufu, which featured a limestone casing, the Pyramid of Khafre employed a combination of red granite for the lower levels and limestone for the upper levels. This stark contrast in materials gives the Pyramid of Khafre an unmistakable appearance, making it appear larger than the Pyramid of Khufu.

Moreover, the satellite pyramid adjacent to the Pyramid of Khafre showcases a simpler structure compared to its counterpart. With two entrances—one at the ground level and another positioned thirty-eight feet above the pyramid's base—this design indicates the builders' intentions to streamline the internal structure, perhaps to avoid the challenges encountered during the construction of the Pyramid of Khufu. Passageways interconnect the entrances, leading to the burial chamber, which now contains an empty red granite sarcophagus. The absence of mummies or relics within the chamber suggests that it may have fallen victim to theft in ancient times.

The statue of Khafre, currently exhibited at the Egyptian Museum in Cairo, stands as one of ancient Egypt's most significant surviving sculptures. The statue depicts the king seated on a throne and bears hieroglyphs that symbolize Khafre's duty to rule Egypt as a unified state.

The Pyramid of Khafre at Giza. If you see a picture of all three pyramids together, you might think the middle pyramid is the tallest, but the Pyramid of Khafre was actually constructed on slightly higher ground.

The Pyramid of Menkaure

The Pyramid of Menkaure is the smallest of the pyramids at Giza, but it is by no means insignificant. Extensive studies reveal that this extraordinary structure boasts a base measuring 356 feet (108.5 meters) on each side, with a height of 215 feet (65.5 meters). However, such dimensions pale in comparison to the colossal Pyramid of Khufu, the largest of the three pyramids.

What sets the Pyramid of Menkaure apart are the intriguing additions adorning its southern side: three smaller pyramids, often referred to as satellite pyramids. These enigmatic structures, though diminutive in scale, contribute to the mystique and allure of the Pyramid of Menkaure.

Venturing further within the pyramid's interior, one encounters an intricate network of passages, leading intrepid explorers to an antechamber and a sacred burial chamber. The entrance to this hallowed edifice lies nestled at a low level, barely above the ground's surface, tempting seekers of knowledge to unveil the secrets hidden within.

Archaeologists discovered a sarcophagus with human bones within the Pyramid of Menkaure. This remarkable find was attributed to the renowned British soldier and Egyptologist Howard Vyse, who, in the 19th century, made an indelible mark on our understanding of Egypt's past.

However, fate dealt a cruel blow to this sarcophagus, as tragedy struck during its journey to England. In an unfortunate turn of events, the vessel entrusted with its safe passage, the *Beatrice*, succumbed to the whims of the treacherous sea, capsizing in 1838. The once-magnificent sarcophagus, destined to grace the halls of scholarly inquiry, met a tragic end, lost to the depths of the ocean.

This sarcophagus was not Menkaure's final resting place, as the sarcophagus held the bones of a woman. His coffin also had human bones in them, but testing revealed they were not old enough to be his. You can see the lid of his coffin in the British Museum today.

The reduced scale of the Pyramid of Menkaure, at least when compared to the grandeur of its counterparts, continues to baffle scholars. The reasons behind this architectural disparity have ignited heated debates among experts, each proposing their own theories to unravel the mysteries of the past. Some conjecture that the confines of the Giza Plateau left little room for the construction of another grand pyramid, while others delve into the realm of politics and economics, suggesting that Menkaure's reign was plagued by issues that prevented the construction of a larger pyramid.

As we tread upon the hallowed grounds of these awe-inspiring structures, the echoes of a lost era beckon us, urging us to unravel the perplexing secrets of the past.

The Pyramid of Menkaure was the third and smallest pyramid built at Giza.

The Great Sphinx

The Sphinx held a revered position as the steadfast guardian of the pyramids and the pharaohs interred within their sacred confines. It embodied the pharaoh's unwavering power and indomitable strength, a resplendent symbol woven into the tapestry of the Giza Plateau.

Interestingly, the term "sphinx," a name of Greek origin, carries a duality of meaning, hinting at both the notion of a "strangler" and the concept of being "constricted." Curiously enough, the Egyptians did not employ this particular appellation. Instead, depictions of the sphinx can be found in diverse artworks scattered across the ancient Middle East, Greece, and even India, forging a connection that spans continents and civilizations.

The Great Sphinx, in particular, assumes the form of a mythical creature, melding the regal countenance of a pharaoh with the commanding body of a lion. Legend intertwines itself with history, as some say that the face of the Great Sphinx bears an uncanny resemblance to Pharaoh Khafre, who is often regarded as its illustrious creator. However, a parallel narrative exists, proposing that Djedefre, in an act of filial reverence, constructed the monument in homage to his father.

The origin of the Sphinx traces back to the very bedrock of the Giza Plateau, as ancient architects hewed and shaped its enduring form with unwavering determination. Successive generations contributed layers upon layers of limestone blocks to restore the monument's weathered façade. However, as the years passed, the Great Sphinx bore witness to the ravages of time, suffering the loss of its once-proud nose, an enigma that has intrigued countless minds throughout the centuries.

Within the realm of lore, a tale once flourished suggesting that Napoleon Bonaparte, in a moment of audacious conquest, fired a fateful shot that severed the nose from its sculpted face. Yet, the brushstrokes of historical truth render this narrative a mere tale, for paintings predating the French invasion depict the Sphinx in its impaired state. Another popular account recounts the actions of a Sufi Muslim who became disenchanted by the locals' veneration of the Sphinx. This man defaced the monument, fervently believing that no image should be worshiped.

The exact circumstances of how the nose was damaged remain shrouded in uncertainty. Archaeological investigations indicate that its disappearance occurred sometime between the 3rd and 10th centuries CE, likely succumbing to the relentless forces of weathering and erosion.

A colossal entity, the Great Sphinx has a staggering length of approximately 240 feet (73 meters). During the annual spring equinox, a celestial spectacle unfolds, as the radiant sun descends majestically over the Sphinx's broad shoulder, casting an ethereal glow upon it.

The Great Sphinx located in front of the Pyramid of Giza in Egypt.
Taken by the uploader, w:es:Usuario:BarcexEspañol: Tomada por w:es:Usuario:Barcex, CC BY-SA 3.0 <http://creativecommons.org/licenses/by-sa/3.0/>, via Wikimedia Commons; https://commons.wikimedia.org/wiki/File:Great_Sphinx_of_Giza_-_20080716a.jpg

Materials That Were Used to Build the Pyramids of Giza

The pyramids of Egypt stand as testaments to human ingenuity and architectural prowess. These remarkable structures, which are considered among the most impressive achievements in history, were constructed with a range of materials and techniques.

R. O. Faulkner, an esteemed English Egyptologist, shed light on the widespread use of limestone in pyramid construction. This versatile stone, with its fine texture and remarkable properties, served as the backbone and outer façade of the pyramids. The inner causeways and wall coatings featured white limestone obtained from locales like the Mokattam Hills, near modern-day Cairo.

Transporting the rough limestone cores posed a formidable challenge. Local quarries provided the necessary supplies, but for the coveted white limestone used, the Egyptians had to venture further. Delving deep into the earth, they meticulously excavated tunnels, plunging up to 160 feet below the surface. The resulting blocks were meticulously cut into smaller pieces. These blocks would be loaded onto sleds that animals or perhaps men dragged through the sand. It is also possible that blocks were loaded onto ships.

While limestone prevailed as the principal material of the ancient pyramids, the Egyptians also used pink granite and basalt. Pink granite, renowned for its durability and aesthetic allure, was a rarity found only in select southern Egyptian locations. The arduous journey from the quarries at Aswan brought this prized stone to construction sites. Similarly, basalt, known as alabaster, occasionally graced the pyramid floors. It was extracted from open pits or hidden underground deposits.

Mud bricks played a significant role in pyramid construction as well. Blending mud and water, the Egyptians fashioned these bricks into a rectangular shape, baking them in the sun's warm embrace. As the rays warmed the bricks, they solidified into a resilient form. To further enhance their durability, the bricks went into an oven.

Through their masterful use of various materials, the ancient Egyptians triumphed over the limitations of their era. Even though they didn't have advanced technology, they were able to overcome their limitations and create structures that could truly pass the test of time.

The Construction of the Pyramids

The pyramids have fascinated people for centuries, but in many ways, they are still shrouded in mystery. The pyramids at Giza, for instance, showcase remarkable technological achievements that continue to astound archaeologists and academics.

According to the accounts of Herodotus, an ancient Greek historian, the construction of the pyramids might have required a staggering 20 years and the labor of 100,000 individuals. However, more recent research suggests a smaller workforce of approximately twenty thousand workers and support staff who managed to complete the construction within two decades. Excavations in the vicinity have unearthed evidence suggesting that the workers were well nourished and supported by the government, with resources likely procured from other Egyptian cities as part of a national endeavor to demonstrate wealth and power.

Historical records indicate that the responsibility of selecting the ideal construction site for the pyramid, as well as managing the personnel and resources, fell upon the vizier, the second highest-ranking official in Egypt. Hemiunu, believed to be Khufu's nephew and the mastermind behind the design and construction of the Great Pyramid, likely acquired his technical expertise from his father, Nefermaat, who was Khufu's brother. The choice of Giza as the location for the pyramids was based on the plateau's ability to support the weight of these colossal structures, as pyramids built on sand would deteriorate more rapidly.

While extensive evidence in the form of bills, logbooks, letters, and articles suggests the completion of the Great Pyramid happened during Khufu's reign, the explicit details regarding its construction are scant. Numerous theories and recent findings provide different explanations for the construction process, yet the knowledge and specialized equipment required to build the Great Pyramid according to its precise design continue to pose a significant barrier to understanding its creation.

One prevalent theory proposes the use of ramps. A ramp would have been constructed around the base of the pyramid and progressively elevated alongside its construction. However, this theory encounters various challenges, including the scarcity of wood in Egypt, rendering the construction of numerous ramps implausible. Moreover, the angle at which the workers would have needed to push the stones upward appears physically impossible without the aid of something akin to a modern-day crane.

French architect Jean-Pierre Houdin put forth a modified ramp hypothesis, suggesting that the ramps were situated inside the pyramid. According to his theory, the ramps would have been used for the pyramid's exterior during the initial stages of construction, with the structure's interior being completed at the same time. The stones transported from the quarry would have been carried up the ramps to their designated spots. This explanation could account for the presence of shafts within the pyramid, but it fails to address the labor requirements or the immense mass of the stones.

Another intriguing theory posits the use of hydraulic power. The high water table beneath the Giza Plateau, where the pyramids stand, is believed to have played a crucial role in this. The Egyptians employed a tool called a shaduf, consisting of a long pole with a bucket, a rope, and a counterweight, to extract water from wells. It is hypothesized that the hydraulic force from below, in combination with hoists situated above, could have been employed to move the stones within the pyramid.

Renowned Egyptologist Zahi Hawass confirmed the challenges posed by the high water table during excavations. Geological studies indicate that the Giza Plateau and its surroundings were more agriculturally inclined during the Old Kingdom since the water table was higher. Thus, it is plausible that the Giza laborers would have constructed the pyramid more efficiently by harnessing the force of the high water table rather than relying on external ramps or other means.

Regardless of the diverse hypotheses proposed, the alignment of the southeastern tips of the three pyramids, alongside the presence of mortuary temples and causeways connecting them, stands as a testament to the high level of planning and organizational capabilities employed during the construction process.

Who Were the Builders of the Pyramids?

Recent scholarly research challenges the widely accepted notion that Hebrew slaves were involved in the construction of the pyramids at Giza, as there is no concrete evidence to support this assumption. While some have turned to the Book of Exodus for support, ancient records do not substantiate the claim that Hebrew slaves were present in ancient Egypt.

Ancient Egyptians held the belief that civic duty and participation in the construction of public monuments, including pyramids, temples, and cemeteries, were essential in honoring the pharaoh and the gods. Therefore, it is believed that the government hired farmers and other laborers to work on these structures during the annual flooding of the Nile River. The Nile's annual flooding, a vital aspect of Egyptian life, deposited fertile soil across the coastal agricultural areas. However, this flooding rendered farming impossible, prompting the government to employ these farmers in other projects. These laborers were responsible for transporting stones and erecting obelisks, temples, and pyramids.

Archaeological excavations shed light on the working conditions of employees involved in the construction of the Pyramid of Giza. These workers received exceptional medical care, had access to food supplies, and consumed approximately four thousand pounds of meat daily, sourced from sheep, goats, and calves. This is supported by the abundance of animal remains discovered in the area. Additionally, the skeletal remains of laborers found in tombs exhibit signs of dental work and expert repair, further substantiating the notion that these workers were well-cared for.

Overseers were employed to supervise the construction process. While documentation regarding the education and knowledge of these overseers is limited, they were tasked with managing the workforce and ensuring the completion of projects to a high standard.

By analyzing this research, it becomes apparent that the construction of the pyramids at Giza did not rely on Hebrew slaves, contrary to popular assumption. Instead, the involvement of farmers and laborers, who were provided with favorable working conditions, seems more likely.

The Great Pyramid as a Tomb

The construction of the Great Pyramid, which is one of the most iconic and well-known structures in the world, was a monumental undertaking. The ancient Egyptians believed the pharaohs needed a grand tomb to serve as a bridge between the gods and the mortals.

Ancient Egyptians were deeply concerned about the welfare of the soul in the afterlife, and this can be observed in the tombs that have been discovered in Egypt, from the simplest to the most extravagant, such as the tomb of Tutankhamun. These tombs have given us extensive evidence, such as engravings and paintings. The Pyramid Texts were funerary texts found in the pyramids of the pharaohs, and they were very prominent during the Old Kingdom. These texts were essentially spells that helped ease people's transition to the afterlife.

Despite the Great Pyramid's grandeur, there has been some debate over whether it was actually used as a tomb. This argument is based on the fact that no mummies or grave goods have yet been discovered. However, it is important to note that grave robbery has been a documented problem in Egypt for centuries.

Egyptologists suggest that the pyramid was looted for artifacts as early as the New Kingdom (c. 1570–1069 BCE), possibly due to the declining importance of Giza as a royal necropolis and the preference for the Valley of the Kings as the favored burial ground for pharaohs.

This does not mean that Giza was completely overlooked during the New Kingdom. There is evidence that pharaohs, such as Ramesses II, better known as Ramesses the Great (r. 1279–1213 BCE), had a keen interest in the area. Rameses II, an influential pharaoh, displayed his reverence for the majestic Great Sphinx by erecting a modest temple right before it. However, his fourth son, Khaemweset, embarked on a mission to safeguard and preserve this sacred site for future generations. Khaemweset, who is hailed as the world's first Egyptologist, dedicated his life to unraveling the secrets of Giza, tirelessly documenting, meticulously restoring, and fervently safeguarding these ancient monuments from the ravages of time.

Herodotus wrote that the Great Pyramid had been looted in the 5th century BCE. In more recent times, visitors can access the pyramid via the so-called "Robbers Tunnel," which was supposedly constructed around 820 CE by Caliph al-Ma'mum in an attempt to gain access to the wealth hidden inside. Throughout history, tomb raiders have frequently targeted the pyramid, and it is likely that any valuables that might have been present during Khufu's and his immediate successors' rule were removed at some point.

While the debate over the purpose of the Great Pyramid continues, it is clear that the ancient Egyptians placed great importance on the construction of grand tombs for their pharaohs. The Great Pyramid, which is the largest tomb of all, was likely believed to serve as the pharaoh's eternal home in the afterlife. The fact that grave goods and mummies have not been discovered within the pyramid should not necessarily be taken as evidence that the pyramid was not used as a tomb.

Mummification in Ancient Egypt

Pyramids and mummies are likely the first things to come to mind for many people when discussing ancient Egypt. The close association between these two elements is not incidental since mummies were frequently entombed in pyramids. The ancient Egyptians held the belief that mummification was intimately connected with the afterlife and the rebirth of the body. This belief was based on their observations of natural phenomena, such as the sun's movements and the life cycles seen in grains and lunar phases.

Ancient Egyptians believed that as long as there was order and the proper requirements were met, the body would be able to survive in the afterlife.

The Pyramid Texts, which date back to the Old Kingdom, suggest that mummification was seen as a necessary process for preserving the body. Based on these texts, chaos engulfed the cosmos when the deity of the underworld, Osiris, met his demise. The essential components for embalming his body, such as resin, incense, and honey, were said to have been formed from the tears shed by the gods.

Before the development of mummification techniques, the bodies of the deceased were simply thrown into pits and covered with sand in the hopes that the dry desert climate would aid in preserving them. However, as burial practices became more elaborate, with the use of mud brick linings and wooden coffins, the bodies began to deteriorate rapidly. To counteract this, the internal organs were removed, and the body was treated with mummifying substances.

Mummification was a common practice from 2400 BCE to the Greco-Roman era. By the time of the Ptolemaic dynasty (the last ruling dynasty of Egypt), mummification had become affordable for most people. Initially, it was believed that only pharaohs could achieve eternal life through mummification, but by 2000 BCE, it was thought that anyone could access the afterlife as long as their body was properly mummified and the necessary objects were buried with them.

However, this was a luxury that was only affordable to the wealthy. The poor would still be mummified, but the process was much simpler. The very poor would be buried in the hot desert sands, which would dry out their body. The body would be covered with natron, a combination of something called soda ash and baking soda, and then covered with some wrappings. The body would be buried in a shallow grave with some personal objects. In the early days, most commoners could not afford to be mummified.

As the mummification process evolved, natron became the primary substance for drying out corpses. The bodies of the elite were tightly wrapped in linen and left for thirty-five to forty days to dry out fully. The internal organs were extracted, treated with dry natron, and carefully stored within canopic jars. These containers were safeguarded by the four sons of the deity Horus. After thoroughly dehydrating the body, it was filled with sawdust, lichen, mud sourced from the Nile, and fragments of cloth to enhance its flexibility. The face was covered with a mask, and the body was further adorned with amulets and other funerary items.

It should be noted that the mummification process was not a requirement for resurrection in the afterlife, but it was widely believed to be the best course of action. Prayers from the *Book of the Dead*, a funerary text popular in the New Kingdom, were often used to help guide the deceased to the next life.

The Arabic term *mumiya*, which means bitumen, is where the English word "mummification" originates. Bitumen, a type of pitch, was used in the early stages of preservation in the Late Period.

Mummification was an important aspect of ancient Egyptian culture and belief, with the process evolving over time. The primary substances used in mummification were sawdust, lichen, beeswax, resin, natron, onions, Nile mud, and frankincense. The body was cleaned and wrapped in as many as thirty-five layers of linen before being submerged in resins and oils, which gave the skin a pitch-black appearance. If the deceased came from a poor family, their family would provide the funeral cloth, which was typically made from old bedsheets or used clothing. The organs were removed, and the cranial cavity was filled with resins via a funnel. The face was oftentimes masked, either with cartonnage (a plaster made from papyrus and water) or gold and silver, the latter of which was mainly reserved for royalty.

Embalmers used a specific set of tools during the mummification process. These instruments consisted of an oil jar, a funnel, bronze rods with hooks for extracting the brain, an embalmer's knife for making an incision in the abdomen, and a wooden tool resembling an adze, used to remove the internal organs. These items were often left in the tomb or nearby once the process was complete[1]. The end goal of mummification was to preserve the body for the afterlife, as it was believed that the soul would return to the body. Mummification was a long and complex process, but it was considered a sacred duty and an essential aspect of

---

[1] There isn't a definitive answer as to why the embalmers left their tools behind. However, it's possible that they left them as offerings to the gods or as a way to aid the deceased in the afterlife. The items could also have been left as a sign of respect for the dead or as a way to commemorate the mummification process. It's also possible that the items were simply left behind due to practical reasons, such as the difficulty of transporting them out of the tomb.

society in ancient Egypt.

Abandonment and Discovery

Between the years 2181 and 2040 BCE, during the First Intermediate Period, Giza was deserted and gradually deteriorated until the Middle Kingdom (approximately 2040-1782 BCE) era. The rulers of the Middle Kingdom vandalized and looted temples, tombs, and pyramids, claiming sculptures for their own construction endeavors. However, during the period of the New Kingdom pharaohs (1570-1069 BCE), a shift occurred, as they devoted themselves to the restoration of Giza.

In 30 BCE, Rome conquered Egypt after the Battle of Actium, and the reverence of the Great Pyramid of Giza and other smaller pyramids, temples, buildings, and tombs were lost. The site remained mostly disregarded until Napoleon's Egyptian campaign, which lasted from 1798 to 1801. Napoleon was interested in the legends of the pharaohs, so he dispatched a team of academics and scientists to catalog the monuments and culture of ancient Egypt. Napoleon's efforts led to a large number of tourists being drawn to Egypt, which, in turn, prompted more people to conduct research and excavations.

British archaeologist Sir William Matthew Flinders Petrie is primarily responsible for the pyramids of Giza's excavation, as he provided a detailed and accurate survey of the pyramids in the early 1880s. His efforts laid the groundwork for all subsequent excavations, and he took great care to ensure the historical accuracy of the artifacts he discovered. His desire to learn everything about the Great Pyramid without endangering the structure established rules to protect and maintain Egypt's historic monuments. It might shock you to learn this, but archaeologists in the 19th century did quite a bit of damage to the sites they explored. They used dynamite and other methods that are frowned upon today.

Archaeological discoveries, even those that damaged the sites, revealed the grandeur and magnificence of the ancient Egyptian civilization's craftsmanship, such as the empty sarcophagus of a queen adorned with furniture and jewelry. Additionally, the presence of mastabas, flat-roofed structures often found in royal tombs that were organized in a grid pattern around the pyramids, suggests the site was a thriving social and commercial center, with artifacts potentially moved to Giza from other parts of ancient Egypt and the eastern Mediterranean. These findings suggest that the focus of study should not be solely on how the pharaohs died but also on how they lived. The pyramids and the hieroglyphics written on the walls of the tombs provide insight into the languages and cultures of the past.

Using 21ʳ-century Technology to Bring the Dead Back to Life

In recent years, advancements in technology have allowed for non-invasive examinations of mummified remains. By utilizing equipment like CT scans, MRIs, X-rays, and endoscopic cameras, researchers are able to gain detailed information about the mummies without causing any damage to the remains. This has allowed for a greater understanding of the mummification process and provides information about the person's gender, age, general health, and method of mummification. Furthermore, analysis of the soft tissue extracted from the mummies has revealed important biological details, such as DNA, genetic markers, and disorders.

Summary of Events

- 27th century BCE: The Saqqara Step Pyramid for Pharaoh Djoser was designed by Imhotep. It was the first pyramid built in Egypt.

- c. 2575-2551 BCE: Pharaoh Sneferu constructed Egypt's first true pyramid, known as the Red Pyramid.

- c. 2550 BCE: The Great Pyramid of Giza was completed by Pharaoh Khufu (also known as Cheops by the Greeks).

- c. 2558-2532 BCE: The second pyramid complex at Giza, the Pyramid of Khafre, was completed.

- c. 2532-2503 BCE: The third pyramid complex at Giza, the Pyramid of Menkaure, was constructed.

Chapter 2 - The Hanging Gardens of Babylon

Babylon, the Gates of the Gods

"When the lofty Anu, King of the Anunnaki, and Bel, lord of heaven and earth, he who determines the destiny of the land, committed the rule of all mankind to Marduk, the chief son of Ea; when they made him great among the Igigi; when they pronounced the lofty name of Babylon; when they made it famous among the quarters of the world and in its midst established an everlasting kingdom whose foundations were firm as heaven and earth – at that time, Anu and Bel called me, Hammurabi, the exalted prince, the worshiper of the gods, to cause justice to prevail in the land, to go forth like the Sun over the Black Head Race, to enlighten the land."

-The Code of Hammurabi

The Code of Hammurabi holds immense historical importance. Hammurabi, the sixth monarch of the Amorite dynasty, governed Babylon from 1792 to 1750 BCE, displaying his dominance as the ruler of Sumeria, Acadia, and the surrounding territories. During his reign, the city-state of Babylon underwent a remarkable transformation, evolving into a formidable empire that encompassed Mesopotamia. Its vast territories stretched from Kurdistan to the Persian Gulf. Babylon's dominance even surpassed that of the formidable Assyrian capital of Nineveh.

In ancient Sumeria, Babylon was renowned as Ka-dingirra, the revered "Gateway of the Gods." According to biblical accounts, it was established by Nimrod, who was the descendant of Cush, the grandson of Ham, and the great-grandson of Noah. The city's gates, named after deities like Shamash, Ishtar, Marduk, Adad, Enlil, Zababa, and Uresh, served as a testament to its rich spiritual heritage. The construction of the legendary Ishtar Gate took place during the reign of Nebuchadnezzar II, the second king of the Chaldean dynasty. This colossal entryway led to the sanctuary of Marduk and served as a fortified enclosure controlling the passage to the northern part of the city. It also housed one of the Seven Wonders of the Ancient World: the Hanging Gardens of Babylon, which were commissioned for Amytis, the queen consort of Nebuchadnezzar II.

Shifting back to the era of Hammurabi, the Amorite ruler left behind a legal legacy known as the Code of Hammurabi. This ancient legal code was likely influenced by earlier law codes, including those of Ur-Nammu, Eshnunna, Bilalama, and Lipit-Ishtar of Isin. Inscribed on a towering stele that stood at a height of eight feet, the code consisted of three hundred laws. Adorning the top of the stele is a bas-relief depicting the sun god Shamash delivering the laws to Hammurabi. Below this intricate portrayal are the laws themselves, inscribed in Akkadian cuneiform script. They encompassed a broad spectrum of subjects, including the establishment of equitable pricing and remuneration, civil and judicial protocols, and penalties for various transgressions.

Regrettably, the stele encountered chaos. Around 1200 BCE, Babylon suffered from looting during invasions led by the neighboring kingdom of Elam. The Code of Hammurabi was taken as a trophy to the city of Susa by King Shutruk-Nakhunte. It remained hidden until its rediscovery in December 1901 by a French archaeological expedition. The stele was then transported to Paris, where it currently resides in the Louvre Museum. Its presence there serves as a testament to the wisdom and legal systems of ancient times.

In the early 20th century, archaeological excavations of Babylon's ruins began. Between 1902 and 1914, German archaeologists conducted extensive digs that unearthed remnants of the magnificent Ishtar Gate. The fragments discovered were transported to Berlin, where a meticulous reconstruction of the gate took place within the Pergamon Museum. Today, visitors have the opportunity to marvel at the restored Ishtar Gate, which is an example of the grandeur and architectural accomplishments of the ancient Babylonian civilization.

Introduction: The Hanging Gardens of Babylon

The Ishtar Gate was not the only magnificent structure created during the Babylonian Empire. According to Greek poets, the Hanging Gardens of Babylon were constructed by King Nebuchadnezzar II around 600 BCE near the Euphrates River (modern-day Iraq). The monument, which may have reached a height of seventy-five to eighty feet, was built primarily to appease the king's beloved wife, Amytis, because she missed her beautiful home in Media (western Iran).

Another legend suggests that Queen Sammu-ramat (Semiramis in Greek), who ruled circa 811 to 806 BCE, may have built the gardens, which were possibly located on the rooftop of the palace. A study conducted between the 20th and 21st centuries argues that the Hanging Gardens may have thrived on rooftops or terraced ziggurats. However, scholars aren't sure who exactly built the gardens; some believe they never even existed.

There are no extant Babylonian records that discuss the Hanging Gardens. However, there are early accounts of the gardens, although there is no evidence that these writers saw the wonder with their own eyes. The earliest written account of the Hanging Gardens of Babylon comes from Berossus, a Babylonian priest who recorded his thoughts around 290 BCE. Later, Greek writers, such as Strabo and Diodorus Siculus, both of whom were active during the 1st century BCE and possibly the 1st century CE, also mentioned the gardens. Even though the gardens were written about many centuries after Nebuchadnezzar's reign and by individuals who may or may not have visited Babylon, various accounts describe the Hanging Gardens as if the author were there. For instance, the geographer Strabo (c. 64 BCE–c. 23 CE) represented the gardens as being close to the Euphrates and flowing through Babylon.[2]

Diodorus Siculus claims that the terraces reached heights of sixty-five feet and sloped upward, showcasing an old auditorium. There are reports of vast gardens documented in Mesopotamia before Babylon was believed to house the gardens if they even existed in the first place.

Furthermore, some academics argue that the Hanging Gardens were not built by Nebuchadnezzar II but by King Sennacherib of Assyria (r.

---

[2] It is unclear whether the gardens flowed through Babylon or if this is referring to the river. The description given by Strabo only mentions that the gardens were near the Euphrates and flowed through Babylon but does not provide further details.

704–681 BCE) in Nineveh rather than Babylon. These scholars believe that the idea that the Hanging Gardens were in Babylon was a major error, as historical discoveries have revealed that Nineveh was known as "Old Babylon" and was a major center of Mesopotamian civilization before the rise of Babylon.

In fact, Sennacherib was known to have built a personal garden in Nineveh that was considered one of the wonders of the ancient world. Some historians speculate that the stories of the Hanging Gardens might have been inspired by Sennacherib's garden and that later writers mistakenly attributed them to Babylon.

The location of the Hanging Gardens of Babylon remains unknown, but many believe they could have been found on or near the east bank of the Euphrates River, about thirty-one miles (fifty kilometers) south of present-day Baghdad in Iraq. However, this is only a theory, as the gardens have only been described in ancient Greek and Roman literature. Some speculate that the gardens were a product of the imagination of Greek intellectuals and poets, while others believe they were a nostalgically imagined oasis for warriors returning from battle.

Despite the lack of concrete evidence for the existence of the Hanging Gardens, the legend continues to capture the imagination of people around the world. Whether they were a real architectural wonder or simply a product of someone's fantasy, the Hanging Gardens of Babylon remain one of the most enduring and intriguing mysteries of the ancient world.

An illustration of the Hanging Gardens of Babylon by the Dutch artist Martin Heemskerck in the 16th century CE.
https://www.worldhistory.org/image/77/hanging-gardens-of-babylon/

Who Was Nebuchadnezzar II?

During the reign of Hammurabi (r. 1792–1750 BCE), the Babylonian Empire rose to prominence and dominated the towns of Mesopotamia. The first iteration of the Babylonian Empire eventually fell around 1595 BCE with the rise of the Persians. Under the leadership of Nabopolassar (626–605 BCE), the Neo-Babylonian Empire was formed. This empire would expand into new territories and create amazing works of art, particularly in regard to architecture.

According to historical accounts, King Nebuchadnezzar II ruled over the empire from 605 to 562 BCE. It is believed that Babylon, located in modern-day Iraq, was a vast and productive city situated between the Tigris and Euphrates Rivers. Since the Neo-Assyrian Empire had been laid to waste, with the capital of Assyria, Nineveh, being overrun during Nabopolassar's reign, Nebuchadnezzar II was able to focus on training a large and powerful army and constructing war chariots, which allowed him to take control of a significant number of territories.

Nebuchadnezzar II demanded taxes from all his subjects, which was (and still is) a common practice. Around 600 BCE, the king of Judah refused to pay any more taxes to Babylon. In 598, King Nebuchadnezzar II attacked Jerusalem, setting in motion the infamous Babylonian captivity. This event is probably what Nebuchadnezzar II is most remembered for, as many Judaeans became captives of Babylon. Jerusalem was ultimately destroyed after a thirty-month siege, and the Great Temple was razed to the ground.

Despite these violent acts, the Book of Daniel reveals that during Nebuchadnezzar II's reign, Babylon flourished and became the most beautiful city in the world. This was achieved through the construction of enormous palaces and temples, as well as structures known as ziggurats, which were believed to have been used as places of worship.

The Appearance of the Gardens in Historical Works

The Hanging Gardens of Babylon remain a mystery in terms of its origin and construction. However, by studying the accounts of early historians, such as Diodorus Siculus, Strabo, and Philo of Byzantium, a glimpse into the gardens can be obtained. It must be emphasized again that there is no proof these historians actually witnessed the gardens firsthand, but the records are important since they are the only proof we have that the gardens might have existed.

According to Diodorus Siculus, a Greek historian, the entrance to the Hanging Gardens was sloped in a manner similar to a hillside and consisted of multiple tiers, each with its own unique components, increasing in size from tier to tier. The gardens were said to have been constructed with earth piled up on each tier and covered with trees of varying sizes and shapes, providing a mesmerizing spectacle for those who viewed it. Furthermore, it was said that the gardens had water mechanisms in place to draw an adequate supply of water from the river, although the inner workings of these mechanisms were not observable.

Another Greek historian, Strabo, described the size of the gardens as quadrangular, with four plethra (one plethron was equal to one hundred Greek feet) along each side. The foundations of the gardens were cube-like and constructed with vaults that had arched openings. Stairs were used to ascend to the roof terrace.

An engineer and writer named Philo of Byzantium also wrote about the Seven Wonders of the Ancient World. He questioned whether the plants in the Hanging Gardens were cultivated using hydroponic methods. Philo believed that the plants were grown in containers rather than in the ground. He also states that the upper terrace of the gardens was embedded with the roots of the plants, providing a sophisticated agricultural system for its time. The gardens were supported by stone columns and had streams of water that came from elevated sources that flowed through sloped channels, helping to water the entire garden and maintain the plants' moisture levels and overall greenery. The gardens were truly a masterpiece and a fitting tribute to the king who commissioned them.

Flavius Josephus, a Roman historian who lived in the 1ˢᵗ century CE and was familiar with the work of Berossus, a Babylonian priest, offered a different perspective on the Hanging Gardens. In his book *Against Apion*, Josephus stated that King Nebuchadnezzar II built the gardens to make his queen happy, as she was originally from Media and enjoyed being in an area that featured hills. However, this account is only a passing reference, and there is little concrete evidence to support it. Some older works suggest that a Syrian ruler was responsible for building the Hanging Gardens, but again, there is little information regarding the specifics of this construction.

It is worth noting that the exact location and even the identity of the ruler who commissioned the gardens remains a mystery and is still debated among scholars. The accounts of early historians are not consistent and may contain errors or exaggerations. The gardens' water supply and irrigation system are not well understood, and there is debate over how they were able to maintain the plants.

Regardless, the most popular theory remains that the Hanging Gardens were built by King Nebuchadnezzar II to please his wife, Amytis. Irrigation systems, using bitumen, reeds, and lead, were likely used to collect water from the Euphrates and disperse it into the air to support the gardens. The Archimedes screw could have potentially been used, as it lifts materials (in this case, water) from a low point to a high point. However, the Archimedes screw was not invented until around 250 BCE, which means the Babylonians would have come up with their own version and neglected to write it down or use it elsewhere.

The Controversies Surrounding the Hanging Gardens

As you can imagine, historians and archaeologists have long disputed the Hanging Gardens of Babylon. People commonly assume the gardens existed in Babylon during Nebuchadnezzar II's reign, but there is little to no evidence to support this. In fact, there is no mention of the Hanging Gardens in any of the Babylonian literature. Nothing has yet been unearthed during archaeological digs that can be utilized to confirm the existence of the gardens.

During Nebuchadnezzar's reign, stone tablets meticulously describe Babylon, including the palace and its diverse military fortifications. So, it seems odd that there is no mention of the Hanging Gardens. This scarcity of concrete evidence has led some scholars to believe the Hanging Gardens is nothing but a myth.

There are three predominant hypotheses about the Hanging Gardens of Babylon. Firstly, they might have existed solely as an elaborate legend. Within the works of Strabo, Diodorus, Siculus, and Quintus Curtius Rufus, a more romanticized portrayal emerges, with these exquisite gardens bestowing verdancy and awe upon the city of Babylon. The second theory proposes that the Hanging Gardens could have once flourished in Babylon, only to meet their demise during the 1st century CE. Alternatively, these gardens might have originally belonged to Assyrian King Sennacherib. We already explored the notion that the Hanging Gardens could have been constructed in the city of Nineveh, situated on the Tigris River near modern-day Mosul in Iraq. That is a possibility, but it is also possible that Sennacherib, who ruled from 704 to 681 BCE, built a magnificent garden in Nineveh that became conflated with the legendary Hanging Gardens.

The term "Babylon" itself was frequently employed to denote the entire region of Mesopotamia. This usage likely contributed to the confusion surrounding the precise location of the Hanging Gardens. The Greek historians who chronicled the gardens might have been alluding to the general vicinity rather than a specific city when using the name Babylon.

Stephanie Dalley, a British Assyriologist and scholar, argues that the Hanging Gardens of Babylon is the garden mentioned by Assyrian King Sennacherib in his inscriptions. Dalley believes that, over time, the location has been misunderstood and attributed to Babylon, which is a more memorable capital. She also points to the archaeological discoveries of enormous aqueduct networks in the region of Nineveh, as well as inscriptions that point to Sennacherib's garden. The area consists of a network of canals, dams, and aqueducts that span fifty miles and was used to transport water to Nineveh. It also contains water-raising screws that were used to transport water to the upper levels of the gardens.

Assyriologist Laurie Pearce proposed that the Hanging Gardens might have been a military garden, possibly established in the space left by the destruction of Nineveh in 612 BCE. She also suggested that there might have been a variety of herbs and plants growing in the gardens, including garlic, coriander, fenugreek, dill, and a range of tree species, including cedars. However, due to the lack of concrete information, it is impossible to determine the precise types of plants that grew in the gardens, if they even existed at all.

Despite the lack of archaeological evidence for the existence of the Hanging Gardens of Babylon, it is possible that evidence of their existence is buried deep within the Euphrates River and cannot be securely recovered. The flow of the Euphrates River has changed throughout the millennia, so it is possible that any signs of the gardens' existence have been buried beneath the waters of the river.

Additionally, it has been hypothesized that Nebuchadnezzar's name may have been given to the gardens for political reasons and that the actual site of the gardens may have been located elsewhere.

The mystery of the Hanging Gardens may never be fully solved.

An Assyrian wall relief depicting the gardens in Nineveh.
https://commons.wikimedia.org/wiki/File:Gardens_of_Ninevah.png

Historians have also considered the possibility that Alexander the Great's troops, who were known to be impressed by the vast affluence of the thriving metropolis of Babylon, might have exaggerated their experiences and memories of the city upon returning to their homeland. This could have led to the embellishment of stories about the grand gardens, palm trees, and towering buildings of Mesopotamia.

To sum up, the existence of the Hanging Gardens remains a topic of debate among scholars. While some argue that the gardens were a myth or were located in another city, others propose that the gardens existed in Babylon but have yet to be discovered. Further research and archaeological discoveries are necessary to uncover the truth about the Hanging Gardens of Babylon.

Gardens in the Ancient World

The ancient world witnessed the birth of gardens, which originated in the Fertile Crescent, transcending their purpose from mere sustenance to sources of pleasure. This novel concept swiftly disseminated across the sprawling landscapes of the Mediterranean and Mesopotamia, gradually becoming a hallmark of opulence for the affluent. Architects embellished gardens with splendid sculptures, captivating water features, and architectural marvels.

A fascinating trend emerged as artisans adept in the art of fresco techniques began to seamlessly integrate the imagery of gardens into their masterpieces. Vibrant depictions adorned villa walls, conjuring the illusion of stepping into a verdant sanctuary upon entering a room. Notable examples of this artistic fusion can be found in the exquisite frescoes discovered in the ancient city of Pompeii.

The Hanging Gardens of Babylon were not the only gardens to appear in ancient Mesopotamia. One other notable example is the gardens at Pasargadae. Constructed by Cyrus the Great in the Zagros Mountains around 550 BCE, these gardens featured terraces for irrigation, tall walls for shade, and trees grouped together to retain moisture and withstand the harsh winds. The gardens were located near an abundant water supply. The connection between gardens and palaces can also be observed in other ancient cultures, such as China and Mesoamerica, which makes it plausible that the gardens of Pasargadae were located close to a palace. It is impossible for us to know what the Hanging Gardens of Babylon looked like (unless we trust the ancient Greeks and Romans), so examining what other ancient gardens looked like gives us a better idea of what the Hanging Gardens might have looked like.

After Nebuchadnezzar's reign, Babylon continued to develop as a great city under the authority of the Achaemenid Empire (550–330 BCE) and Seleucid Empire (312-63 BCE). It is stated that both empires made frequent use of the palaces in Babylon as their residential palaces. There is a very good chance that the gardens were still in existence many centuries after the structure was completed, as the city was reported to have kept its strategic significance for many years.

In 1899 CE, archaeological investigations in Babylon began to take on a more methodical approach. However, there have been no significant findings of the Hanging Gardens. Nevertheless, other ancient monuments, like the double walls and the Ishtar Gate, were found during excavations. During one excavation, fourteen vaulted rooms belonging to the South Palace of Babylon were uncovered. It is possible that more information on the gardens might be unearthed the more excavations are made.

For instance, excavations were carried out close to the river that gave the impression of the site being the king's palace. These excavations uncovered walls, drains, and something that could be a reservoir, all of which are typical structures for gardens; however, there was no evidence to prove that this location was the Hanging Gardens.

It is difficult to believe that the gardens never existed because their story is so widespread. It is hard to imagine that an ancient scholar came up the Hanging Gardens on a whim, although the possibility cannot be ruled out. If the writer was being meticulous about their work, they would have based their information on something, and it is possible that that "something" has disappeared. Additionally, the Hanging Gardens have been on the list of the Seven Wonders of the Ancient World for a long time. It is also entirely possible that the Hanging Gardens of Babylon should have been called the Hanging Gardens of Nineveh.

Summary of Events

- 605 BCE–562 BCE: King Nebuchadnezzar II reigns as king of Babylon and is credited with constructing the Hanging Gardens of Babylon, at least according to tradition.

- c. 575 BCE: Nebuchadnezzar II constructs the Ishtar Gate and the massive walls of Babylon.

- 225 BCE: The Seven Wonders of the Ancient World is formalized by Philo of Byzantium. The list included the Hanging Gardens of Babylon.

- 1st century CE: If the Hanging Gardens existed, it has been theorized they were destroyed in the 1st century CE. However, they could have fallen into disrepair centuries before.

Chapter 3 - Temple of Artemis

According to Greek mythology, Artemis was said to have ruled over the flora and fauna, fertility, and other natural forces. She was also the goddess of chastity and hunting. The most notable temple dedicated to Artemis, which was known as Artemesium, was located in Ephesus (modern-day Turkey). The temple was rebuilt more than once, with the first temple being built sometime in the 8th century BCE. The current theory is that this temple was wiped out by a flood since the region is prone to flooding. The second, more iconic structure took around 120 years to build.[3]

Construction of the second temple began during the rule of a Lydian king named Croesus (r. 560–546 BCE). King Croesus took over Ephesus sometime between 560 and 550 BCE. After his victory, he started building the Temple of Artemis.

The Roman historian Pliny the Elder, who lived in the 1st century CE, stated that Chersiphron of Knossos built the second reconstruction of the Temple of Artemis, which measured more than 370 feet by 150 feet. However, Strabo believed that Chersiphron had help from his son, Metagenes. Strabo's theory seems more probable, as constructing a temple of this size would have been a massive undertaking. The Ephesians even believed that Artemis built the temple since the temple's blocks above the columns weighed twenty-four tons each.

---

[3] This number comes from Pliny the Elder, a Roman historian, so it is possible the temple did not take this long to build.

Pliny states that when the work site was damp, charcoal seams and sheepskins were layered upon one another. The temple was also reconstructed on the same site as the original since it was believed the location would protect it from earthquakes. It is thought to be one of the largest Greek temples to ever be constructed. It was even bigger than the Parthenon!

According to Pliny the Elder, the temple consisted of 127 columns, each approximately 60 feet in height. Vitruvius, a Roman architect from the 1ˢᵗ century BCE, described the temple as dipteral octastyle, meaning it had two rows of columns around the temple with eight columns on each of the front and back façades. The Ionic columns were said to have Greek mythical figures inscribed on them, and Amazons were painted on the shrine's ornamental mural.

According to Pliny the Elder, the second temple took around 120 years to construct, lasting from 550 to 430 BCE. There are various accounts of the temple's destruction, with one story stating that it was burned down by Herostratus in an attempt to make his name famous. Apparently, Herostratus was sentenced to death because of his actions. People also could no longer speak his name since the authorities did not want his name to be remembered; of course, someone jotted it down as we know his name today.

Herostratus allegedly did this on Alexander the Great's birthday (July 21ˢᵗ, 356 BCE). Another account, this one by Plutarch (born in the 1ˢᵗ century CE), relates to Alexander the Great's birth. According to legend, Artemis was assisting in the delivery of Alexander the Great on that day and was not present at the temple.

According to tradition, in 333 BCE, Alexander the Great visited Ephesus and expressed a desire to sponsor the temple's reconstruction as long as his name was placed on it. However, the leaders were hesitant to engrave his name on the temple. They respectfully declined, saying that it would be inappropriate for the name of one deity to appear beside that of another.

Nevertheless, in 323 BCE, the temple was rebuilt, with Macedonian architect Dinocrates playing a role in the reconstruction. He worked diligently to restore every aspect of the once-majestic structure. The temple housed an array of artistic treasures, including a captivating portrait of Alexander the Great painted by the celebrated artist Apelles.

The temple served as a hub for pilgrims for centuries. However, the Ostrogoths attacked the city in 262 CE. They sacked the temple. Some sources say it was not rebuilt, so the temple must not have been completely razed since people still used it. However, it would never reach its former glory again. In 380 CE, Christianity was acknowledged as the official state religion of the Roman Empire (of which Ephesus was part), and about ten years later, Emperor Theodosius outlawed paganism and declared all pagan temples should be shut down. It is believed that the temple was destroyed by Christian believers in 401 CE. It would not be rebuilt again.

There are various accounts of the Artemesium's destruction. According to the Acts of John (a collection of stories about the Apostle John), John issued a death threat to the general populace and prayed to God for forgiveness on account of the people's foolishness. As a result, the altar of the Temple of Artemis fractured into a great number of pieces. The statues of more than seven gods were shattered into a thousand pieces, and the temple's ceiling collapsed, resulting in the death of a priest.

There are also reports from the Syriac *History of John*, which indicates that the priests recanted their beliefs and beat their faces with grief. They walked away from the altar, went to John, and prostrated themselves in front of him. After that, they wrapped ropes around the statue of Artemis and toppled it. However, the most likely explanation is that Christians tore down the temple, which was likely already lying in ruins, in the early 5th century CE.

The Temple of Artemis was included on the list of the Seven Wonders of the Ancient World after it was built for the second time. This is what the site looks like today.

Who Is Artemis?

Artemis, also known as Diana in Roman mythology, holds a significant place in Greek lore as the twin sister of Apollo. Revered as the patroness of hunters and wild animals, she is often depicted with her iconic bow and arrow. Artemis, one of the revered twelve Olympian deities in Greek mythology, presided over an array of domains, including nature, the moon, chastity, hunting, and childbirth.

As the daughter of Leto and Zeus and the twin sister of Apollo, Artemis fiercely protected her virginity and the purity of her priestesses. Iconic portrayals often depicted her as a youthful huntress astride a stag or another majestic creature, brandishing her bow. Despite her role as a guardian of women and young girls, Artemis was not associated with procreation, and her narratives frequently emphasized the importance of chastity.

Throughout Greece, shrines and temples devoted to Artemis were scattered far and wide, with renowned sanctuaries gracing locations like Brauron and Karyai. Artemis's stories, such as transforming her hunting companion Callisto into a bear or her plea to Asclepius to resurrect Hippolytus after he pledged to lead a celibate life, further underscored her fervent dedication to safeguarding the purity of her priestesses and her detachment from fertility worship.

Interestingly, the first Temple of Artemis, constructed by the Ionians, was believed to be situated in Ortygia, near Ephesus, rather than on the renowned island of Delos. This temple, dating back to the 8th century BCE, unfortunately met its demise due to a devastating flood in the 7th century BCE. Recent archaeological discoveries have shed light on this catastrophe, yet the fate of the original temples remains shrouded in mystery.

According to legend, the statue of the goddess Artemis, which held a special place of worship within the temple, was discovered by Amazons hailing from northern Turkey. However, additional details are required to validate the accuracy of this tale and to unravel the circumstances surrounding the construction of the initial temple. The remaining sculptures of Artemis in Ephesus portray her standing with her knees together and arms outstretched in front of her, elegantly adorned in a long skirt adorned with animal motifs.

It is believed that Artemis of Ephesus was influenced by other deities, such as Isis and Cybele, showcasing the profound impact of local beliefs and customs on the development of Greek religion. Beyond her role as the goddess of fertility, Artemis held the esteemed position of the city's guardian. As the temple's popularity grew, an influx of tourists and devout followers of Artemis brought lavish offerings of jewelry and financial contributions, significantly bolstering the city's coffers. Ephesus eventually became renowned as a sanctuary for individuals seeking refuge from persecution. Even the Amazons supposedly made two separate journeys to the city in search of solace.

Where Was the Temple of Artemis Located?

The convergence of Greek and local cultures is exemplified in the ancient city of Ephesus, located near the modern Turkish city of Selçuk. This region has been inhabited by humans for millennia, but the city's prominence rose during the early Bronze Age. However, it was not until the 11th or 10th century BCE that the city was called Ephesus. Despite this, the local inhabitants continued to exert significant influence. A prime example of this cultural blending is the unification of the Greek goddess Artemis and the regional fertility goddess Cybele. Scholars believe the site of the Temple of Artemis was a sacred place devoted to the veneration of the mother goddess since the Bronze Age.

The Ionians established the ancient city of Ephesus in the 11th or 10th century BCE. It was located at the base of Ayasuluk Hill in present-day Turkey and served as a prominent trade hub in the eastern Mediterranean.

Throughout the majority of its existence, Ephesus was a port city. Its decline was due to wars and ecological difficulties. The city was situated on the Aegean Sea at the mouth of the Kaystros River, which emptied into a bay. However, sediment slowly filled the river, obstructing harbor access. Because of sediment buildup, Ephesus was relocated five times. As time went on, the region around the city became sandier, and it is now receding from the ocean.

The location of the renowned Temple of Artemis faced issues of frequent flooding and marshy conditions as early as the 8th century. A previous worship center dedicated to Artemis was destroyed by devastating floods.

Relics of the Temple of Artemis

The revered Temple of Artemis showcased magnificent statues skillfully crafted by artists, although the original bronze masterpieces have regrettably been lost to the ravages of time. Nevertheless, reproductions created during the Roman era offer a glimpse into the appearance of these statues. They portrayed a majestic female figure of similar height, stature, and attire, often with her right arm gracefully raised above her head or occasionally resting on a spear.

The artifacts mentioned in this section primarily pertain to the later Temple of Artemis (the one on the list of the Seven Wonders of the Ancient World), which began construction sometime around 323 BC. The earlier two builds of the temple have limited surviving evidence.

The Lady of Ephesus.
Gargarapalvin, CC BY-SA 4.0 <https://creativecommons.org/licenses/by-sa/4.0>, via Wikimedia Commons; https://commons.wikimedia.org/wiki/File:Efes_M%C3%BCzesi,_2019_11.jpg

Within the esteemed halls of the National Archaeological Museum of Naples, one can encounter an Ephesian worship statue that dates back to the 2nd century CE. This particular statue deviates from the commonly associated Roman representation of Diana, showcasing the deity adorned with a modius (a headdress), meticulously crafted from alabaster and bronze and positioned atop her head. Furthermore, the statue incorporates depictions of breasts, eggs, or perhaps the testicles of sacrificial bulls, symbolizing ideas of fertility and abundance. Another modius from the later temple is currently on display at the Museo del Palazzo dei Conservatori in Rome.

The pediment, the triangular gable adorning the front of the later temple, is believed to have featured three windows or apertures, likely depicting intricately adorned scenes. It is speculated that one of the bronze statues depicting the Amazons might have been positioned in this area. However, only fragments of the pediment have withstood the test of time, leaving the full image of the Temple of Artemis shrouded in mystery.

A model of the third Temple of Artemis located in Istanbul, Turkey
Zee Prime at cs.wikipedia, CC BY-SA 3.0 <http://creativecommons.org/licenses/by-sa/3.0/>, via Wikimedia Commons https://commons.wikimedia.org/wiki/File:Miniaturk_009.jpg

The later Temple of Artemis, which was extensively explored and excavated by John Turtle Wood with the invaluable support of the British Museum during the late 19th century, has yielded remarkable discoveries, including the temple's foundation and an immense column drum. Wood's six-year quest culminated in the unearthing of the temple's buried pavement in 1869. Situated approximately twenty feet below the marshy terrain, the excavation of the pavement necessitated the acquisition of the entire property to ensure cost-effectiveness. Extracting the pavement alone would have entailed significant expenses.

During the meticulous excavation process, an enormous column drum weighing over eleven tons was discovered in September 1871. The drum was partially submerged in water and inverted. Wood employed his expertise to restore the column drum to its original position by constructing supporting columns and elevating it. After two arduous months of work, the marble drum was cautiously wrapped and prepared for transportation to the British Museum. Twenty dray horses were used to transport it!

Upon closer scrutiny of the six feet by six feet marble drum, scholars noticed intricate carvings of a woman, potentially representing Alcestis or Eurydice. The figure of Hermes Psychopompus, renowned for guiding spirits to the underworld, was sculpted. He holds a caduceus. The left side of the drum showcased Thanatos, the personification of death, while Persephone and Pluto (or Hades in Greek mythology), the rulers of the underworld, were depicted on the right side. If authenticated as the work of Scopas, one of the illustrious sculptors of that era, this discovery would hold significant artistic and historical significance. Nevertheless, uncertainties persist about the temple, such as whether the structure had an outdoor area or was covered with wooden tiles.

Archaic Temple Adornments.

The embellishments of the older temples are a subject of fascination. It is said that the second temple was an intricate structure with a rooftop that provided shelter to the altar. Recent archaeological discoveries provide evidence of the earlier temples' existence, although information on what the first temple would have looked like is scarce.

The second temple was believed to have been built between the 6th and 4th centuries BCE. The ornate decorations of the temple, consisting of friezes and other embellishments, were located on the lower drums of the columns, the parapets, and the columns themselves. These adornments would have been popular during the Ionic era. Depictions of various animals and horses on some of the pieces of the frieze have been, indicating some sort of procession.

Historians know this version of the temple was important, as more than one thousand objects were left behind at the site dating to this period, including some of the earliest coins in history. Records indicate that it was around 377 feet (115 meters) long and a little over 150 feet (46 meters) wide. It was supposedly built of marble, which would have made it the first

Greek temple made out of that material.

The second temple had a double row of columns that formed a passage around the inner chamber, which would have held an image of Artemis. According to Pliny the Elder, these columns were forty feet (thirteen meters) high and intricately carved.

The Altar

The Temple of Artemis in Ephesus is a fitting location for the grand altar, which measures 39.70 meters in length and 16.67 meters in width. It was shaped like a horseshoe. The Ephesus Archaeological Research Institute unearthed several polygonal or trapezoidal slabs from the ancient temple's soil, which contain remnants of walls on the south, east, and north sides. The Hellenistic temple had a base with 3.4 meters on each side that faced west and was adorned with two rows of columns instead of walls. The priests could ascend the altar via a ramp, thanks to its horseshoe design and elevated position.

The altar was not solely a place of worship but also a separate structure that was part of the larger temple. Given the considerable number of merchants, service providers, refugees, and asylum seekers who visited the site, it is not surprising that the altar stood out from the rest of the temple.

Hellenistic Temple Description

The architectural layout of the third reconstruction of the Temple of Artemis appears to be quite standard, consisting of a stairway running up from the basement to the main building. The main building is believed to have measured around 344 feet (105 meters) in length and around 180 feet (55 meters) in width and features two rows of columns that are almost 60 feet (17.6 meters) in height. The sculptures and bas-reliefs that decorated this temple were similar to those seen in other ancient temples.

The actual structure of the building had a rectangular outline. However, the exterior of the walls did not take the form of a giant rectangle but rather two smaller sides that were set at a lower level. This resulted in the formation of a naos, or sanctuary, on the side of the entrance and a posticum, or back room, on the side facing away from the entrance.

Despite having a rectangular shape, the hall was broken up into three distinct portions. A roof that was supported by four columns could be found above the vestibule, which was found just behind the entrance. The temple's treasury could be found on the left side of the building, while the steps were found on the right. The cella, also known as the main room (the room where the image of the goddess was placed), was situated in the middle of the building.

What Happened to the Temple?

As mentioned, the first version of the temple was likely destroyed in a flood. The second version was burned down by Herostratus. Some believe that he might not have set fire to the temple, though. To truly destroy the temple via burning, he would have had to set fire to the wooden roof. Doubters of him being the culprit find it unlikely that no one stopped him, especially considering the temple was well guarded. Another theory is that the temple administrators purposefully set the temple on fire since it was sinking and needed to be rebuilt.

The third temple became disused as time passed. Christianity rose in popularity, with the traditional Greek and Roman religions being abandoned. In 262, the Goths sacked the temple. Since Artemis was no longer worshiped as much as she had in the past, it is likely the temple sat in its derelict state until Christianity became the official religion of the Roman Empire. It is possible that a Christian mob destroyed whatever was still standing of the building in 401 CE.

Some of the stones of the Temple of Artemis were used to construct other buildings, but it is not known for sure what buildings were built on the foundation of one of the Seven Wonders of the Ancient World. Some say the Hagia Sophia contains stones from the temple, but this seems highly unlikely.

The Impact of the Temple of Artemis

The Temple of Artemis transcended its role as a mere site of worship. Historical records attest to the temple serving as a bank. Its strategic positioning permitted it to be somewhat removed from the machinations going on in Ephesus, which allowed it to stay dedicated to the reasons it was created in the first place. The Temple of Artemis in Ephesus was also used for a very long time, considering it was built in the Bronze Age and still had worshipers visit during the Roman Empire. The veneration of Artemis of Ephesus proliferated across the Aegean Sea, Anatolia, the Mediterranean Basin, and even the Iberian Peninsula.

The portrayal of Artemis of Ephesus was unparalleled in comparison to other representations of the goddess. The esteemed custodian of the temple, known as the *megabyse*, wielded authority on par with the magistrates of Ephesus during the peak of the temple's influence. The Temple of Artemis also acquired a reputation that forbade any desecration or intrusion by other factions, including the Lydians, Athenians, Persians, and Spartans. Not even the formidable Alexander the Great could assert dominion over the sacred grounds.

Summary of Events

- 7th century BCE – The first Temple of Artemis was destroyed, likely by a flood.

- c. 550 BCE – The reconstruction of the Temple of Artemis began in Ephesus.

- 356 BCE – The Temple of Artemis was destroyed by a fire.

- 323 BCE – The Temple of Artemis was rebuilt yet again.

- 2nd century BCE – Antipater of Sidon includes the Temple of Artemis on his list of the Seven Wonders of the Ancient World.

- 262 CE – The Temple of Artemis was plundered by the Goths.

- 401 CE – The Temple of Artemis was possibly destroyed by a Christian mob. If this did not occur, then the temple was destroyed in some other way.

Chapter 4 - The Statue of Zeus

The Statue of Zeus stood in the ancient world for almost one thousand years in the sanctuary of Olympia, located in the Peloponnese Peninsula. It is believed that the statue oversaw the ancient Olympic Games. The first Olympic Games are believed to have been held in 776 BCE and were considered a significant event in the history of Greece, with the date of the games and the name of the first foot-race winner, Coroebus of Elis (who was a cook), being widely known among the Greek population.

Who Was Zeus?

Zeus, known as Jupiter in Roman mythology, was the supreme deity in Greek and Roman mythology. His multifaceted nature and the diverse roles he played made him a figure of great importance.

Firstly, Zeus was regarded as the god presiding over the air. He possessed the power to unleash storms and tempests. This portrayal emphasized his dominion over the forces of nature, showcasing his ability to command the elements and inspire awe in the hearts of mortals.

Secondly, Zeus personified the laws of nature and embodied the unchanging and harmonious order that governed the physical and moral realms. As a deity associated with the laws of the universe, he represented the immutable principles that regulated the natural world and the conduct of individuals. His influence extended beyond the mere physical realm and encompassed the moral fabric of society.

Furthermore, Zeus was revered as the guardian of state life and the progenitor of kingly power. He played a crucial role in the establishment and preservation of political institutions, symbolizing the fundamental authority that underpinned the governance of states and the rule of kings. The Greeks looked upon Zeus as their protector, recognizing his importance in maintaining stability and order within their communities.

Lastly, Zeus held the esteemed position of being the father of gods and men. As the divine patriarch, he assumed the responsibility of overseeing the actions and well-being of both deities and mortals. His paternal role signified his concern for the welfare of all beings and highlighted his involvement in the affairs of the celestial and earthly realms.

Greek mythology is replete with numerous myths and stories surrounding Zeus, each contributing to the intricate tapestry of his character. One particularly well-known myth revolves around Zeus's upbringing. According to the tale, Zeus was concealed by his mother, Rhea, to safeguard him from his father, Cronus, who harbored fears that one of his offspring would overthrow him. Raised in secrecy on the island of Crete, Zeus eventually returned to dethrone Cronus and ascended as the ruler of the gods.

Another popular myth involving Zeus is the narrative of the flood. Disillusioned by the corruption and wickedness among humanity, Zeus decided to send a deluge to wipe out all the mortals. Yet, he spared Deucalion and Pyrrha, a righteous couple, who were instructed to repopulate the earth by casting stones over their shoulders, which miraculously transformed into human beings.

These stories serve as a testament to Zeus's immense power, authority, and active participation in the affairs of gods and humans. They exemplify his capacity to influence the course of events, showcase his role as a moral arbiter, and underscore his commitment to the dispensation of justice. Overall, Zeus was venerated and worshiped by the Greeks for his dominion over the natural world, his guidance in matters of state, and his paternal concern for the well-being of mortals.

The Temple of Olympia: Pre-Statue of Zeus

Olympia, nestled in the enchanting region of Elis within the sprawling western Peloponnese Peninsula, welcomed weary souls embroiled in the labyrinthine web of Greek factions locked in perpetual conflict. Seeking solace and security, people flocked to this idyllic haven. And in Olympia, an unparalleled spectacle unfolded—the inaugural Olympic Games, which became an ode to human prowess and camaraderie.

A stadium served as the stage for these momentous games and their accompanying festivities, while the Altis, a sanctuary within the city, flourished with magnificent temples.

In 590 BCE, a temple honoring the sacred bond between Hera and Zeus was built. Hera, the goddess of femininity and childbirth, was the wife of Zeus, the mighty deity presiding over lightning, thunder, and life-giving rain. These divine figures, the quintessential king and queen of all Hellenic gods, were celebrated at the Temple of Hera, the oldest temple in Olympia. Their sculpted forms were enshrined within the sanctified walls of the temple. Hera was seated regally beside Zeus, who stood as her steadfast guardian. Once the Temple of Zeus was built, he was no longer worshiped as much at this temple, allowing Hera to become the predominant one.

Within the sacred confines of this celestial sanctuary, ancient flames danced upon the altars of old. Today, the Olympic flame is lit within its ruins, still illuminating the past and present. The temple was destroyed sometime in the early 4th century CE due to an earthquake.

Sometime in the 5th century BCE, a little over a century after the inception of the Temple of Hera, the seeds of a new temple were sown. A symphony of artistry and craftsmanship sprouted, birthing the Temple of Zeus, a monument that would command reverence and admiration for generations to come. This architectural masterpiece finished construction in 456 BCE. It stood tall, an epitome of beauty and wonder.

Inside the temple, a colossal statue of Zeus reigned supreme, its sheer magnitude dwarfing mortal comprehension. Honored as one of the Seven Wonders of the Ancient World, this divine effigy imbued the sanctum with an awe-inspiring aura.

Thus, Olympia remains etched in the annals of history, not only because of the famed Olympic Games but also because of the people's reverence and architectural creations.

The Temple of Zeus

In the 5th century BCE, Olympia experienced much prosperity, as it was a time when grandeur and ambition melded seamlessly. It was during this era that the construction of a colossal Doric temple with a six-by-thirteen column layout commenced. The Eleans, enriched by their triumph against the Triphylians, generously financed this monumental undertaking. A mastermind by the name of Libon of Elis shepherded the project to completion in 456 BCE. Libon's crowning achievement, the Temple of Zeus, is renowned far and wide and is believed to have provided inspiration for the illustrious Parthenon that would grace the

Athenian landscape in later years.

The Temple of Zeus, an imposing rectangular edifice oriented from east to west, boasted an array of sculptures and other embellishments that dazzled the people who visited it. Accounts relayed by Pausanias, a distinguished Greek geographer and writer of the 2nd century CE, describe a towering structure reaching a lofty height of 68 feet (21 meters) and stretching 95 feet (29 meters) wide and 230 feet (70 meters) in length. This magnificent temple proudly displayed thirteen columns on its elongated sides and six columns on its shorter sides. Crafted from local limestone and adorned with a white plaster coating, these columns provided support for the resplendent white marble roof.

The temple's interior embraced a minimalist aesthetic, a canvas of simplicity designed to elevate the awe-inspiring centerpiece—the Statue of Zeus. Built around 435 BCE, this sculpture commanded attention, casting a spell of reverence upon all who set foot within the temple. While the interior exuded restraint, the exterior walls depicted tales of Greek mythology on the pediments, the triangular spaces above the doorway. The eastern pediment narrated the thrilling chariot scene from the tale of Pelops and Oenomaus, while the western pediment immortalized the legendary clash between the Lapiths and the Centaurs. Some of these remarkable pieces of art still exist today, serving as enchanting relics and guardians of timeless legends begging to be retold.

To truly unravel the intricate tale of Oenomaus and Pelops, one must first explore the narrative of Tantalus, Pelops's ill-fated father. Born of Zeus and the nymph Pluto's divine union, Tantalus wielded immense power and basked in the gods' favor as the ruler of Phrygia. However, his hubris and insolence led him astray, as he dared to betray the deities by serving his own son in a feast to the immortal beings as a way to test their powers.

Swift retribution descended upon Tantalus, with the gods banishing him to the depths of Hades, consigning him to eternal torment for his transgressions. However, a glimmer of mercy shone through Zeus, as he was moved by compassion for the tragic Pelops. One of the Fates resurrected the young prince, although he was missing a piece of his body, his shoulder, which had been eaten by one of the gods. An ivory prosthetic replaced the missing shoulder. Pelops fled to the sanctuary of Pisa after being unseated by King Ilus of Troy, setting the stage for a fateful encounter.

Within the realm of Pisa, Pelops found himself entangled in the destiny-shaping web of King Oenomaus, the proud father of the captivating maiden, Hippodamia. The king devised a treacherous chariot race, a daring test of skill and courage, with the hand of Hippodamia as the coveted prize. Thirteen suitors had already met their tragic end trying to win her hand.

Unfazed by the inherent danger, Pelops embraced the race with unyielding confidence, a conviction borne from his divine equine companions and the benevolence of the gods. Guided by the clandestine aid of Hermes and the king's own charioteer, Myrtilus, who covertly tampered with Oenomaus's chariot, Pelops emerged triumphant. The king's ill-fated vehicle careened off course, sealing his own tragic fate.

As the conqueror of the race, Pelops claimed Hippodamia as his beloved bride. In gratitude for Myrtilus's assistance, Pelops rewarded the charioteer. Yet, consumed by insatiable greed, Myrtilus yearned for more, conspiring to orchestrate Pelops's downfall. Their tumultuous conflict reached its climax with the fateful demise of Myrtilus, who cursed Pelops and his progeny.

This curse cast a long, ominous shadow over the House of Atreus, culminating in the tragic saga of Agamemnon and Clytemnestra. Nevertheless, Pelops succeeded in establishing a powerful dynasty in Pisa, forever intertwining his name with the origins of the illustrious Olympic Games.

As one wandered through the hallowed halls of the Temple of Zeus, one couldn't help but be transfixed by the pivotal moments of Pelops's extraordinary journey. Today, the temple's intricate sculptures, including metopes, which fill the space between triglyphs (the ends of the wooden beams holding the roof), portraying the legendary Hercules undertaking his mighty labors, can be admired at the Olympia Museum.

An illustration of what the Temple of Zeus might have looked like. This illustration was made in the early 20ᵗʰ century.

Master Sculptor Phidias

In the vast and ancient realm of Greece, where history intertwines with myth and legends, Olympia stood as a jewel cherished by the polis of Elis. Its magnetic allure drew in visitors from near and far, from wide-eyed tourists seeking adventure to devout pilgrims in search of spiritual solace. Olympia also attracted sports enthusiasts who traveled from all corners of the Mediterranean to witness the exhilarating competitive games held there.

Olympia sought to become a place where gods and mortals converged, a nexus of divine energy that would leave a mark on the annals of history. At the heart of this endeavor stood Zeus, the supreme ruler of the Olympian gods, a towering figure whose influence permeated every aspect of the religious and cultural fabric of ancient Greece.

To honor and appease the mighty Zeus, a monument of his glory was deemed necessary—an offering that would encapsulate the collective devotion and awe of the Greek people. So, the esteemed Phidias, a visionary among mortals, was bestowed with the responsibility of bringing this ambitious vision to life. With unparalleled craftsmanship and boundless creativity, Phidias embarked on a journey that would alter the course of Olympia's destiny.

In the 20ᵗʰ century CE, a flurry of excavations took place; it was as if the earth itself yearned to reveal the secrets buried within its bosom. During this meticulous unraveling of time's tapestry, an astonishing discovery emerged—an intricate workshop, a testament to Phidias's tireless labor. Within the fragmented remnants of the workshop, several treasures of the past, such as tools and materials, emerged. Most noticeably, archaeologists found a red-figure Attic cup delicately adorned with the words *Pheidio eimi* ("I belong to Phidias"); however, many historians believe the inscription to be a forgery.

Phidias's creative genius was not a solitary endeavor; it took a team of skilled craftsmen and artisans, each contributing their unique talents. As Phidias carefully set his plans in motion, the temple's interior became a sanctuary for artists. With meticulous precision, the ivory and gold plates were shaped and polished, melding together to form the statue's lifelike skin. Zeus wore a crown of olive leaves and donned a robe made of glass. According to Pausanias, who detailed the sculpture in vivid detail, the robe was covered with lilies and animals. The king of the Olympians held a statue of Nike, the goddess of victory, in one hand, and in the other was a scepter. The statue, a majestic, seated figure towering at an impressive twelve meters, was meticulously fashioned by Phidias using a striking combination of ivory and gold.

Of course, a king needs a throne. The Statue of Zeus, which measured around forty feet (twelve meters) tall, sat on an immaculate throne decorated with gold, ivory, and other precious materials. Panaenus, Phidias's brother, is thought to have been the one who painted the throne. The floor in front of the statue was paved with black tiles, and there was a pool of oil, which was used to help keep the ivory in pristine condition.

According to legend, Phidias was so overcome once he finished that he prayed to Zeus, asking if his work was good enough. A lightning bolt struck the floor, signifying Zeus's delight with the sculpture. Those who saw the statue say that it was one of the most awe-inspiring things they had witnessed. For instance, Livy said the Roman general Aemilius Paullus is said to have been "moved to his soul, as if he had seen the god in person."

Alas, even the mightiest of mortals can succumb to the fickle winds of fate. Phidias went on to create another amazing work of art, the *Athena Parthenos*, in the Parthenon. However, once the work was completed, Phidias was accused of stealing money. It is likely the charges were false, as he was very close with Pericles, the ruler of Athens. Pericles had many enemies, so it is very plausible that the charges were made up to get back at Pericles.

Phidias supposedly tried to prove his innocence by showing that the gold he had stolen was actually used in the *Athena Parthenos*. But another charge appeared in its place. He had placed his image and that of Pericles on Athena's shield, which would have been viewed as blasphemy. This charge was likely to be true. Phidias was placed in prison, where he died.

Though the Statue of Zeus itself has been lost to the unforgiving currents of time, it is still remembered in history as one of the Seven Wonders of the Ancient World. Fragments of the grand Temple of Zeus still stand, weathered by time, while remnants of Phidias's workshop provide a glimpse into the inner workings of a mastermind.

The legacy of Phidias lives on, not just in the remnants of Olympia but also in the countless replicas that dot the Mediterranean landscape.

The most accurate reproduction of the Athena Parthenos.
Photo by George E. Koronaios, cropped by Neoclassicism Enthusiast, CC BY-SA 4.0

What Happened to the Statue of Zeus?

Once majestically towering over the picturesque Greek Peloponnese Peninsula, the Temple of Zeus served as a sacred space for worship. Athletes from all over would gather every four years on this hallowed ground, paying homage to the gods, making offerings to Zeus, and pledging their commitment to fair play before engaging in the competitions. The temple played a significant role in honoring Zeus and facilitating the grand athletic festivities that captivated participants and spectators.

According to Roman historian Suetonius, Roman Emperor Caligula, who reigned from 37 to 41 CE, wanted the Statue of Zeus to be relocated to Rome since the statue was so grand. However, he also wanted to take off Zeus's head and replace it with his own. This story might not be real, but this next part is pure fiction. When Caligula died in 41, the statue apparently knew, as it burst into laughter, causing the scaffolding to crumble.

Although Caligula did not bring about the statue's end, it did meet a gruesome fate. Like the Temple of Artemis, Christianity played a large role in the temple's and statue's demise. In 393 CE, Emperor Theodosius I issued a decree banning the Olympic Games. There is archaeological evidence that the games continued, although they were not as grand as they once were. That changed under Theodosius II, who was even more ruthless in rooting out paganism. He ordered the destruction of the Temple of Zeus in Olympia in 426 CE.

It takes a lot to ruin a grand temple, though, and it is likely pieces of it still stood after the dust had fallen and the flames had subsided. Whatever was left would have been affected by the earthquakes that shook the land in 522 and 551 CE. After a bad flood, the area was abandoned, with silt and other organic materials burying the temple. The Temple of Zeus wouldn't be remembered by history until 1766 when Richard Chandler, an English historian, identified it. Excavations of the site would take place around sixty years later.

The statue would not have been as hard to tear apart as the temple itself. But it is hard to know for sure what exactly happened to it. In 391, Emperor Theodosius I banned pagan worship and closed the temples. People might have taken advantage of that order to tear the statue apart, with pieces of it being melted down to sell. It might have been torn apart and carted off to somewhere else where it was put back together.

Historians once believed it was taken to Constantinople, where it was later destroyed in a fire in 475.

If it wasn't removed prior to the temple's destruction in 425, the statue would have been destroyed then. And if that was the case, it likely was destroyed by people who fervently believed in Christianity or the emperor, or it burned in the fire.

The Temple of Zeus at Olympia, once a shining symbol of religious devotion and a venue for grand athletic celebrations, now exists merely as ruins. Nevertheless, the memory of this extraordinary temple and the captivating Statue of Zeus it sheltered continues to ensnare the imagination and inspire artists today.

An illustration of the Statue of Zeus.
https://commons.wikimedia.org/wiki/File:Le_Jupiter_Olympien_ou_l%27art_de_la_sculpture_anti que.jpg

Summary of Events

- 776 BCE: First athletic games take place at Olympia to honor Zeus.

- c. 456 BCE: The Temple of Zeus at Olympia is constructed.

- 435 BCE – The Statue of Zeus is created by Phidias. This masterpiece is recognized as one of the Seven Wonders of the Ancient World.

- 225 BCE: Philo of Byzantium documents the Seven Wonders of the Ancient World, which included the Statue of Zeus at Olympia.

- 395 CE: The statue of Zeus at Olympia is supposedly relocated to Constantinople.

- 426 CE: Emperor Theodosius II orders the destruction of the Temple of Zeus at Olympia.

- 475 CE: The Statue of Zeus is destroyed in a fire in Constantinople.[4]

---

[4] It must be noted that there is no firm proof of what happened to the Statue of Zeus. This is just one of the theories.

Chapter 5 - The Mausoleum of Halicarnassus

The Mausoleum of Halicarnassus, also referred to as the Tomb of Mausolus, was a shrine dedicated to Mausolus and his wife and sister, Artemisia II of Caria (present-day Turkey). This relationship was out of place, as there is no mention of Carian rulers practicing incest. Some scholars believe the marriage was symbolic, especially since the two never had children. Mausolus and Artemisia II served as governors (satraps) in the Persian Empire.

Who Was Mausolus?

Mausolus was a Persian satrap in the region of Caria, situated in the southwestern part of Anatolia. His rule lasted from either 377 or 376 to his demise in 353 BCE. He was born in Caria and fostered an ambitious vision of elevating his domain to the status of an expansionist power, prompting him to relocate his capital from Mylasa to the coastal city of Halicarnassus.

Intriguingly, Mausolus played a pivotal role in the momentous revolt staged by the Anatolian satraps against the formidable Persian king Artaxerxes II. Yet, demonstrating an astute sense of timing, Mausolus wisely withdrew from the conflict before succumbing to defeat. This maneuver allowed him to preserve his autonomy as a ruler and further solidify his influence over the territories under his sway.

Notably, Mausolus incorporated fragments of Lycia and several Ionian Greek cities into his expanding domain. In an act of strategic alliance, he provided support to the islands of Rhodes, Cos, and Chios in their struggle against mighty Athens, culminating in their resounding victory. Consequently, Rhodes and Cos fell under Mausolus's sphere of influence, further augmenting his political power.

Halicarnassus blossomed into a thriving capital city under Mausolus's guidance. Driven by a vision of impregnable security, he undertook extensive fortification projects, constructing formidable defensive walls, watchtowers, and three distinct walled citadels. These architectural endeavors served as a testament to his sagacity and tangible manifestations of his unwavering commitment to safeguarding his realm.

Mausolus's reign bore witness to a unique dynamic, as he shared the reins of power with his sister and wife, Artemisia II. This arrangement was unconventional, to say the least. There is no mention of incest being popular in Caria, and it seems unlikely the two ever consummated their marriage. Artemisia also held some power, even though she herself was not referred to as a satrap. Together, the couple steered Caria and its neighboring territories through twenty-four eventful years.

In regard to the subject of this section, Mausolus initiated the construction of an awe-inspiring sepulcher that would subsequently be known as the Mausoleum of Halicarnassus, a marvel listed among the Seven Wonders of the Ancient World. Upon his demise, Artemisia assumed the mantle of overseeing the completion of this grand tomb, which featured larger-than-life depictions of the Carian king and queen. This architectural project was a collaborative effort conceived by Greek architects named Pythius and Satyrus (also spelled as Satyros) and embellished by the masterful hands of esteemed Greek sculptors like Scopas, Bryaxis, Leochares, and Timotheus.

Mausolus left an enduring legacy that extended far and wide. He is known for being a tyrannical ruler by the Greeks he ruled, but his territorial expansions brought Caria unprecedented growth, while his unwavering support for commerce and fortification engendered prosperity and security. His steadfast promotion of Greek culture and literature fostered an atmosphere of intellectualism within his domain.

The term "mausoleum" became an enduring testament to Mausolus, with the term being used to refer to any imposing burial structure. Although the physical remnants of the mausoleum now lie in ruins, the profound impact of his reign on Caria and the splendor of his architectural masterpiece continue to mesmerize historians and visitors alike.

Who Was Artemisia II?

Artemisia II acted as a ruler, patron, and scholar. She was born circa 395 BCE as the eldest daughter of Hecatomnus, the first of his line as a Carian satrap. Her other siblings included Mausolus, Ada, Idrieus, and Pixodarus. Ada and Idrieus would also marry each other, likely to solidify Idrieus as the next satrap of Caria, similar to Artemisia II and Mausolus.

Artemisia played a pivotal role in consolidating her family's claim to a relatively autonomous Caria while honoring the overarching authority of the Persian Empire. Collaborating with her husband Mausolus, she masterfully thwarted Athenian imperial aspirations embodied in the Second Delian Confederacy, safeguarding Caria's cherished autonomy.

Tragedy struck Artemisia's life with the demise of her husband and brother in 353 BCE, compelling her to devote the remainder of her existence to immortalizing his memory. It is likely that Mausolus had already planned a grand tomb to be built, but Artemisia was the one who saw it come to life. She oversaw the construction of Mausolus's mausoleum, an opulent burial complex that would grace the city of Halicarnassus (modern-day Bodrum, Turkey). This architectural marvel, revered for its grandeur and splendor, ascended to the prestigious ranks of the Seven Wonders of the Ancient World, magnetizing travelers with its allure.

The profound grief that enveloped Artemisia's heart following her husband's passing permeated her every breath until her own demise in 351 BCE. It is even said that she drank her brother's ashes because she was so distraught. She hired poets to praise his name, and she ensured the mausoleum would be finished to honor Mausolus's greatness.

Her reign as Caria's sole ruler endured a mere two years, culminating in her brother Idrieus and sister Ada jointly ascending to the throne. The mantle of power was then passed on to their younger brother, Pixodarus, in 340 BCE.

Beyond Artemisia's political triumphs, she also explored the realms of botany and medicine. She engaged in research and garnered some acclaim. In fact, a drug used to help treat malaria, Artemisinin, was named after the plant Artemisia annua, which was named after Artemisia II.

Artemisia II is remembered as a devoted spouse, influential ruler, and revered patroness of the arts who bequeathed an enduring legacy through the magnificent Mausoleum of Halicarnassus. Her indomitable spirit and unwavering dedication continue to resonate with people today, making the study of the Mausoleum of Halicarnassus all the more interesting.

An Architectural Marvel: The Mausoleum of Halicarnassus

The construction of the mausoleum, situated in Halicarnassus (present-day Bodrum, Turkey), took place between 353 and 350 BCE. This impressive structure, reaching an estimated height of approximately 148 feet (45 meters), was the collaborative effort of two Greek architects, Satyrus and Pythius. Adding to its grandeur, five renowned Greek sculptors of the time, Bryaxis, Leochares, Scopas, Timotheus, and Pythius (who was also involved in crafting the chariot), contributed to the design of each of its four sides.

Halicarnassus was founded by the Dorians, with its origins dating back before 1100 BCE, although historians have not reached a consensus on the exact founding date. By the time Mausolus assumed power, the region had undergone significant changes. It was no longer a Dorian colony but had become part of the vast Persian Empire. Despite this, Mausolus, who inherited the position of satrap of Caria from his father in 377 or 376 BCE, embraced Greek customs and governance. He transformed Halicarnassus into the new capital and worked diligently to showcase Greek architecture. Mausolus constructed streets and buildings for the local population and fortified the port with impressive structures. These efforts brought about substantial improvements to the city, including the creation of ports, a palace, and numerous temples, which stimulated trade in the eastern Mediterranean and bolstered the city's economy. Halicarnassus is also famous for being the birthplace of the renowned historian Herodotus, who was born in the 5th century BCE.

While Mausolus undoubtedly revitalized the city and expanded his influence, he was not universally regarded in a favorable light. Some individuals branded him a tyrant or despot due to his authoritarian rule. In 353 BCE, Mausolus passed away, leaving Artemisia II devastated. To honor her late husband, Artemisia decided to move ahead with his plans to erect an extraordinary tomb. Despite facing a rebellion from the Greek island of Rhodes following Mausolus's death, Artemisia managed to secure the necessary funds and dispatched five exceptional sculptors to oversee the construction of the tomb. Regrettably, Artemisia died a mere two years later, shortly before the mausoleum was finished. Both of their remains were interred within the incomplete mausoleum. This hilltop structure, adorned with stone lions and soldiers, featured thirty-six columns.

Tragically, the mausoleum's fate took a turn when a series of earthquakes struck between the 12th and 15th centuries CE, reducing it to ruins. The remnants of this once-majestic monument were later repurposed in the construction of other buildings, including the castle built by the Knights of Saint John, also known as the Knights Hospitaller. Nevertheless, fragments of statues and slabs from the mausoleum have found a new home in the British Museum in London, England.

Even today, grieving families continue to erect mausoleums as eternal resting places for their departed loved ones. Perhaps the most renowned mausoleum worldwide, and incidentally one of the Seven Wonders of the New World, is the Taj Mahal.

A model of what the Mausoleum of Halicarnassus might have looked like.
Jona Lendering, CC0, via Wikimedia Commons;
https://commons.wikimedia.org/wiki/File:Mausoleum_at_Halicarnassus_at_the_Bodrum_Museum_of_Underwater_Archaeology.jpg

So, What Did the Mausoleum Look Like?

The Mausoleum of Halicarnassus was an imposing edifice built to serve as the final resting place for Mausolus and Artemisia. It radiated an air of exceptional grandeur and lavishness. Its dimensions, though not precisely known, can be deduced from historical accounts and archaeological discoveries that attest to its colossal and opulent character.

Perched on a stone platform nestled within a courtyard, the mausoleum was adorned with an array of sculptures, including statues depicting gods, goddesses, and lions. The central tomb, shaped like a truncated pyramid, ascended in the form of a nearly square cube, measuring approximately 126 feet by 106 feet (38.4 meters by 32.5 meters). Adorning the base of the structure was an intricate bas-relief frieze, displaying intricate artistry.

Enclosed within a protective barrier, the mausoleum featured an east-facing chamber, serving both as a functional vestibule and a symbolic threshold between the realm of the living and the domain of the departed. This demarcation of the temporal and spiritual realms through dedicated spaces was a customary practice in antiquity and carried deep cultural significance.

Thirty-six columns provided support to the mausoleum's roof, with ten columns adorning each side and one gracing each corner. These columns matched the height of the roof, which took the form of a pyramid, complete with twenty-four steps. At the pinnacle of the mausoleum, an illustrious quadriga statue commanded attention. A quadriga is a portrayal of four horses pulling a chariot; in this case, the quadriga was possibly transporting Mausolus and Artemisia to the heavens.

Though the exact measurements remain shrouded in uncertainty, historians frequently reference the figures provided by Pliny the Elder, who cited a total perimeter of 411 feet (125 meters). Gaius Julius Hyginus alluded to the mausoleum's resplendent stone embellishments and approximate dimensions as being 80 feet (24 meters) in height and 1,340 feet (410 meters) in circumference.

The interior of the mausoleum housed an expansive collection of sculptures, boasting over four hundred free-standing statues painstakingly crafted by master artists. The walls were adorned with a plethora of reliefs and friezes, displaying diverse aspects of Mausolus's life and the pivotal events of his time. Bearing the influences of Greek culture, these friezes also depicted epic battles between the Greeks and the Amazons, as well as the clashes between the Greeks and the Centaurs.

These extravagant embellishments, epitomized by the larger-than-life statues, would have made the Mausoleum of Halicarnassus truly awe-inspiring, creating an atmosphere of profound reverence and admiration. While its precise measurements may elude us, there is no doubt that this structure stood as a monumental testament to the elevated status and immense power wielded by Mausolus and Artemisia.

An example of one of the friezes that could be found in the mausoleum. This is the Amazonomachy Relief and shows two Amazons, three Greeks, and a horse duking it out.
Carole Raddato; Attribution-ShareAlike 2.0 Generic (CC BY-SA 2.0);
https://creativecommons.org/licenses/by-sa/2.0/;
https://www.flickr.com/photos/carolemage/16897971954/

The Quadriga

As mentioned, the Mausoleum of Halicarnassus was adorned with a massive statue referred to as the quadriga, which sat atop the structure. A quadriga was a type of two-wheeled chariot pulled by four horses. The statue was approximately 21 feet (6.5 meters) in length and stood at a height of around 16.5 feet (5 meters). The quadriga did not remain intact, but fragments of it can still be seen today at the British Museum. One of the fragmented horses has its head lifted high and turned to the left, which imparts a sense of energy and vitality.

One of the horses of the Quadriga of the Mausoleum of Halicarnassus. It became fragmented over the centuries.

https://commons.wikimedia.org/wiki/File:Horse_Halicarnassus_BM_1002.jpg

The horse was intricately carved, as you can see its muscles and veins. Its teeth and tongue were also skillfully carved. The mane covers both sides of the horse's neck, and there is a lock of hair around its right eye. Two strips of a harness wrap around the torso, connecting the collar to the crest of the headgear. Remnants of paint are still visible, and the statue in its modern form was reconstructed using various parts.

It is not known for sure what the quadriga was meant to represent. Some scholars believe that it was inspired by a religious funeral rite. It is believed Mausolus and Artemisia were in the chariot, but it is not known for sure. If the chariot was empty, it is possible it was meant as an offering to Mausolus. This was a rare custom in ancient Greece, but it did occur on occasion.

Since it is more likely that the chariot was occupied, other theories have emerged. It makes sense that the chariot would have been occupied by Mausolus and Artemisia, with the quadriga being made in honor of them. However, it is also possible that the chariot was used by Mausolus and his driver. The Greek goddess of triumph, Nike, was often depicted accompanying a monarch on his way to the afterlife. Some scholars also believe that either the deity Helios or Apollo controlled the chariot.

What Happened to the Mausoleum of Halicarnassus?

Halicarnassus, with the mausoleum nestled within its embrace, bore witness to the relentless dance of earthquakes spanning centuries. The rhythmic undulations of these seismic disturbances inflicted wounds upon the mausoleum, gradually eroding its splendor and leaving behind ruins. The tremors bear the responsibility for the decay and ultimate collapse of the mausoleum. It is unknown if just one massive earthquake damaged the building or if successive earthquakes brought the building down.

In the annals of the 15th century CE, a chapter unfolds where the Knights of Saint John of Rhodes, better known as the Knights Hospitaller (their full name is the Order of Knights of the Hospital of Saint John of Jerusalem), embarked upon the construction of a fortress in Bodrum, melding the remnants of the Mausoleum of Halicarnassus into its fortifications. These gallant knights sought to erect an impregnable bastion, shielding the region from incursions and warding off any aggression.

It is important to note that by the time the Knights Hospitaller repurposed the mausoleum, it had already succumbed to ruin. The ceaseless quakes and the relentless march of time had exacted their toll upon the edifice, rendering it a dilapidated shell. The knights, resourceful as they were, employed the remnants of the once-majestic structure as a veritable quarry, gathering stones and materials to serve their own construction endeavors.

Next, we find ourselves transported to the 1850s CE amidst the excavations conducted under the stewardship of Charles Thomas Newton. Within the bowels of the earth, an opulent trove lay in wait, as countless artifacts and sculptures revealed themselves. Amongst the unveiled treasures were statues of ethereal beauty, frieze slabs that whispered tales of forgotten epochs, and sculpted figures immortalizing the regal splendor of lions and horses. These relics were carefully documented and transported, their journey leading many to find a new home within the halls of the British Museum in London, where they presently reside. These sculptures and other artifacts offer a tantalizing glimpse into the artistry and architectural opulence that once enrobed the mausoleum.

It is worth noting that Charles Thomas Newton narrated a thrilling moment of discovering pieces of a horse statue. This remarkable find sparked an astonishing collaboration between eighty individuals hailing from the region, who valiantly united to transport the piece atop a sturdy sled. The walls encircling the area where this magnificent equine treasure was unearthed bear exquisite paintings.

However, the archaeologists did not find an accompanying chariot. Historical records concerning the discovery in Bodrum do not explicitly mention the unearthing of a chariot alongside the majestic horse's remains.

Yet, the fates of Mausolus and Artemisia, who were enshrined within the mausoleum, remain an elusive riddle. Though it is widely believed that their remains were interred within the sanctum, the precise coordinates of their tombs elude scholars. The earthquakes and the ensuing modifications to the structure have helped to shroud their final resting place. Perhaps their remains were destroyed, or perhaps we will one day discover them.

The castle that arose from the visionary ambitions of the Knights Hospitaller still adorns the landscape to this very day. Today, it is known as Bodrum Castle or the Castle of Saint Peter. Over the course of its existence, this fortress has witnessed numerous changes. Today, the Museum of Underwater Archaeology stands as a testament to the castle's enduring legacy. And there, within the sheltered confines of the castle's bastions, are the remnants of the Mausoleum of Halicarnassus, bridging the chasm between the past and the present and offering a tantalizing glimpse into the resplendence that once graced the city of Halicarnassus.

While the Mausoleum of Halicarnassus now lies as a modest mound of earth adorned with scattered stones and columns, its past grandeur never fails to captivate our collective imagination. This extraordinary architectural marvel rivaled even the famed pyramids of Giza. Its weathered remains stand as a testament to the ingenuity and artistic prowess of ancient civilizations, beckoning us to ponder the mysteries of the past and immerse ourselves in the rich tapestry of Bodrum's storied heritage.

Summary of Events

- 377/376 BCE–353 BCE: Mausolus rules over the kingdom of Caria.

- 353 BCE–350 BCE: Construction commences on the Mausoleum of Halicarnassus, which is intended to be the final resting place for Mausolus and his sister-wife, Artemisia II.[5]

- 225 BCE: Philo of Byzantium becomes the first known historian to mention the Seven Wonders of the Ancient World.

- Between the 12th century and the late 14th century CE: A devastating earthquake strikes, resulting in the tragic destruction of the Mausoleum of Halicarnassus, leaving behind mere remnants of its once-majestic splendor. It is possible that several earthquakes hit the region during this time.

- c. 1494 CE: The Knights of Saint John of Rhodes repurpose sections of the Mausoleum of Halicarnassus in the construction of the walls of Saint Peter's Castle in Bodrum.

---

[5] Many historians think a mausoleum of this size and detail would have taken longer to build. It is possible that its construction began earlier during Mausolus's rule or that later rulers helped finish it.

Chapter 6 - The Colossus of Rhodes

The Colossus of Rhodes embodied the grandeur of Greek mythology and the triumph of the human spirit. This monumental statue, which stood tall as a tribute to the radiant Greek sun god Helios, held a deeper significance rooted in history. Its creation is attributed to the brilliant mind of Chares of Lindos, and it was constructed between 292 and 280 BCE against the backdrop of Rhodes's glorious victory over Demetrius I Poliorcetes. The besieged city emerged victorious in 305 BCE, marking a turning point in its narrative.

Crafted with meticulous artistry, the Colossus of Rhodes left onlookers in awe. As legends tell, this colossal figure reached an astonishing height of approximately 110 feet (33.5 meters). Its core structure, concealed within a blend of bronze and iron, provided the necessary support to bear the weight of the sculpted stone exterior. These details are sadly all that is left of this ancient wonder.

Contemplating the exact whereabouts of the Colossus has also been a matter of intrigue and speculation. While historical records are scarce, the prevailing belief suggests that the statue graced the harbor, commanding the attention of all who approached. This location, a gateway to the thriving city of Rhodes, would have allowed visitors to bask in the awe-inspiring presence of the statue and possibly even sail between its legs as they entered the port city.

However, it is important to note that the accounts we have inherited from the Middle Ages very well might be inaccurate. Myths and legends were intertwined with history, blurring the lines between fact and fiction. So, while the portrayal of the Colossus as a towering sentinel overlooking the harbor evokes some vivid imagery, it is not known for sure if it stood there.

Nonetheless, one cannot dismiss the inherent allure of the Colossus of Rhodes. Even in the absence of precise details, the idea of a colossal monument dedicated to a revered deity speaks to the aspirations and achievements of humanity. Its inclusion among the Seven Wonders of the Ancient World exemplifies the magnitude of its impact and the enduring fascination it evokes.

Where Is Rhodes?

Rhodes, an island nestled in the Aegean Sea, holds a historical gem known as the port of Rhodes. Positioned at the northern tip of this landmass, the port played a pivotal role as a destination along various trade routes. These routes intertwined Greek cities in Asia Minor, such as Miletus, with the resplendent treasures of Egypt. The island of Rhodes itself is a fascinating place, steeped in history and rich in cultural heritage.

The ties between Rhodes and the illustrious city of Alexandria were as strong as the sturdy columns that adorned the magnificent temples of old. The year 331 BCE was a momentous year in history, for that was the year the mighty Alexander the Great established the city of Alexandria. This vibrant metropolis became a beacon of culture and knowledge, captivating the hearts and minds of those who ventured there.

Even in more recent times, Rhodes has continued to captivate visitors with its picturesque landscapes and idyllic beaches. The Old Town, a UNESCO World Heritage Site, stands as a testament to the island's medieval past, with its imposing fortifications, narrow cobbled streets, and charming blend of Byzantine, Ottoman, and Italian influences.

The Rhodian Conflict

The ancient city of Rhodes held a significant position in the realm of commerce, owing to its strategic location along major trade routes. During the reign of Alexander the Great's successors, the Mediterranean region flourished, attracting the attention of influential figures like Demetrius I of Macedon, who was entrusted by his father, Antigonus I, a former comrade of Alexander, to conquer vast territories. When Alexander died, his vast empire fragmented, with his generals fighting for control over it. Antigonus ultimately ruled over Macedonia and its neighboring domains.

In 306 BCE, before assuming kingship, Antigonus dispatched his son, Demetrius, to launch an assault on Ptolemy, another of Alexander's generals who later established his dominion over Egypt. Realizing the need for assistance, Demetrius sought the aid of the Rhodians, but they declined to lend their support. Demetrius still managed to emerge victorious, decimating Ptolemy's forces in the Battle of Salamis and subsequently annexing Cyprus.

This triumph was followed by a succession of coronations. Antigonus and his son declared themselves kings, and they were joined by Ptolemy, Cassander, Lysimachus, and Seleucus I Nicator, all of whom had served under Alexander. With newfound autonomy, Demetrius resolved to punish Rhodes by laying siege to its namesake capital.

Rhodes, the administrative center of the island, found itself encircled by Demetrius, who amassed a force of around forty thousand soldiers and pirates. This number significantly surpassed the city's population, though it should be noted that ancient historians, while our main sources, occasionally embellished facts for dramatic effect or propagandistic motives. Nonetheless, it remains plausible that Demetrius commanded a formidable assembly.

Engineers from far and wide were recruited to conceive and construct a remarkable siege weapon, a towering 125-foot (38-meter) structure equipped with wheels and housing a catapult. To safeguard the catapult operators, leather shutters were installed, and each level of the tower featured its own water tank in anticipation of the city's fiery counterattacks. Pushing this behemoth required over three thousand soldiers, but despite its awe-inspiring design and technological advancements, its effectiveness was nullified by the muddy surroundings caused by residential flooding in Rhodes. Demetrius also possessed an immense 180-foot (55-meter) battering ram, which required the efforts of approximately one thousand men to wield it effectively.

The conflict between Demetrius and the resolute people of Rhodes endured for an entire year until a ceasefire was negotiated. The citizens of Rhodes withstood the siege with unwavering determination, and when reinforcements from Egypt under Ptolemy's command arrived, Demetrius had no alternative but to retreat from the island. Although he considered the siege a triumph due to Rhodes agreeing not to support Egypt in his war against Ptolemy, the tenacity of the Rhodians ultimately prevailed.

In the aftermath, the people of Rhodes found themselves in possession of Demetrius's colossal siege tower and other equipment, which they sold for a hefty profit. They decided to use the funds for the construction of a monumental statue in honor of their patron deity, Helios. And the rest, as they say, is history.

The Colossus of Rhodes

According to Greek mythology, Helios was the son of the Titans Hyperion and Theia and was venerated as the sun god by the Greeks. The Halieia festival, which honored Helios, was one of the most important religious celebrations on the island of Rhodes. The mythology of Rhodes is also tied to Helios through the nymph Rhodos, who was said to have been the mother of his sons.

The Colossus of Rhodes, a 110-foot statue of the Greek god Helios, was built between 292 and 280 BCE. According to Roman historian Pliny the Elder, it took three hundred talents (an estimated five million dollars today) and twelve years to complete the project. It is unknown how many men worked on it, but the number was likely high. The statue had a bronze exterior and an iron framework. It was supported by two or three stone columns inside. The iron framework and stone columns were connected using iron rods.

Helios is typically depicted wearing a crown of sunbeams on silver coins during the Hellenistic period, so it is assumed that the statue bore the same appearance. Although the exact appearance and location of the statue are unknown, it is widely believed to have been located near the harbor. There are detractors to this theory, though. The statue is traditionally believed to have straddled the harbor, with the waterway passing under its legs. There are several remnants around the harbor that could have been the statue (none of which straddle the harbor). Although the idea of the Colossus of Rhodes straddling the harbor evokes a powerful image, it is incredibly unlikely that it did since it doesn't make sense from an engineering standpoint. Additionally, some scholars believe the Colossus of Rhodes was part of the Acropolis of Rhodes, which sat on a hill near the port. However, nothing has been confirmed so far, as there are no firm details of the statue's appearance or location.

Attempts have been made to rebuild the Colossus of Rhodes, with the first proposal presented in the 1970s. However, the rebuilding has been controversial. Some argue that it would boost the tourism industry, while others claim that it would cost hundreds of millions to recreate. In

November 2008, it was announced that the statue would be reconstructed, but the exact height of the sculpture has not been determined. So far, the statue has not been built. One of the most recent proposals was in 2015, but plans have not moved forward.

How Was the Statue Constructed?

Modern architects and scholars widely acknowledge the existence of the Colossus of Rhodes, yet there persists an ongoing debate regarding how it was constructed. Chares of Lindos, a pupil of the renowned sculptor Lysippus, who held the esteemed position as Alexander the Great's personal sculptor, was assigned to the task. Tragically, Chares of Lindos met an untimely demise before completing the project. It is not known for certain how he died, which paved the way for myths and tales to come up with solutions. Some stories suggest that suicide was the cause. According to one account, a Rhodian inspected Chares's work and discovered a flaw that so overwhelmed the sculptor with shame that he resorted to taking his own life. Another story attributes Chares's suicide to his underestimation of the exorbitant cost involved in constructing such a colossal statue, leading him into bankruptcy and despair. However, historical records fail to definitively confirm the exact cause of his demise or whether he passed away prior to the statue's completion, although it is widely believed he died before it was finished.

Speculation also abounds when it comes to the construction method employed for the Colossus of Rhodes. One theory put forth by some scholars posits that Chares of Lindos used a large earthen ramp that expanded in size as the statue grew taller. This ramp would have allowed the workers access to the statue throughout the construction process. However, this idea finds little favor among modern architects, who consider it impractical and unrealistic, given the immense size and weight of the statue.

Constructing the Colossus of Rhodes undoubtedly presented formidable challenges due to its sheer scale and complexity. Unfortunately, no comprehensive records or architectural plans have survived to provide definitive insights into the specific techniques employed. As a result, architects and historians have to rely on ancient accounts and limited archaeological evidence to come up with their own conjectures regarding the construction process.

While contemporary architects continue to put forth theories and ideas, a widely accepted consensus on the construction of the Colossus of

Rhodes remains elusive. The lack of conclusive evidence, coupled with the passage of time, contributes to the enduring mystery surrounding the methods employed in creating this monumental ancient masterpiece.

What Did the Statue Look Like?

The Colossus of Rhodes is indeed a fascinating subject, and while there is no extant description of the statue, there have been various theories proposed regarding its appearance. Based on the available information, it is believed that the Colossus stood approximately 110 feet tall, a number that includes its 50-foot stone pedestal.

The most widely accepted theory suggests that the statue depicted the Greek sun god Helios. It is thought that the statue portrayed a male figure with his arms raised in the air. Similar to the Statue of Liberty, which was erected centuries later, the Colossus of Rhodes is believed to have worn a crown of rays and potentially held a cloth or torch.

As we also mentioned, the location of where the Colossus stood is still a matter of debate. While it is commonly assumed that it was located near the harbor, the exact spot is not well documented. The idea that the statue straddled the harbor, as depicted in Martin van Heemskerck's 16th-century engraving, is now considered a misconception. Such a pose would have been deemed undignified for a god, and the construction required for such a stance would have likely necessitated the closure of the port for an extended period. It is now believed that the Colossus of Rhodes stood with its legs together.

We bring that point up again to highlight the similarities between the Colossus of Rhodes and the Statue of Liberty. Both statues were located near a harbor and depicted figures with raised arms, wearing a crown of rays and holding a torch. However, it is important to note that the Statue of Liberty was not directly inspired by the Colossus of Rhodes. Instead, it was a gift from France to the United States and was designed to symbolize freedom and democracy.

A 16th-century engraving of the Colossus of Rhodes by Martin van Heemskerck, who illustrated all of the Seven Wonders of the Ancient World.

https://en.wikipedia.org/wiki/File:Colossus_of_Rhodes.jpg

While the Colossus of Rhodes no longer exists, it continues to captivate our imagination, and the details of its appearance remain a subject of speculation and scholarly debate.

This engraving was created around 1875 by Sidney Barclay. It gives you another idea of what the statue might have looked like.

https://commons.wikimedia.org/wiki/File:Colosse_de_Rhodes_(Barclay).jpg

The Collapse of the Colossus of Rhodes

The Colossus of Rhodes stood for an impressive span of approximately fifty-six years until a mighty earthquake struck the region in 226 BCE (some sources also suggest it might have fallen during an earthquake in 228 BCE). Legend tells a tale of the Egyptian monarch Ptolemy III extending a generous offer to finance the reconstruction of the colossal sculpture. However, the inhabitants of Rhodes, guided by an oracle's enigmatic counsel, opted to forgo this opportunity.

Their unwavering conviction stemmed from a belief that the imposing statue had, in some way, incurred the wrath of the sun god Helios. In an extraordinary display of reverence, the Rhodians resolved to preserve the shattered remnants of the monument, allowing them to bear witness to the indomitable might of their celestial deity. As a testament to his immense power, the broken fragments of the Colossus lay scattered along the sun-kissed beaches of Rhodes, serving as a poignant reminder of its former magnificence.

The sands of time continued their ceaseless dance, and Rhodes experienced yet another chapter of transformation. In the year 654 CE, the island succumbed to the conquest of the Arab forces, which were led by the future founder of the Umayyad Caliphate, Mu'awiyah I. The chronicles of Theophanes the Confessor, a Byzantine historian of notable repute, narrate a captivating account of a Jewish merchant hailing from Edessa, an ancient city nestled in upper Mesopotamia. According to Theophanes, this astute trader purchased the fractured remains of the Colossus of Rhodes and undertook an arduous journey to transport his valuable acquisition.

Theophanes, ever the weaver of tales, asserts that an astonishing caravan of nine hundred camels bore the weight of this remarkable bounty. Alas, in the realm of historical inquiry, the veil of ambiguity shrouds this story, leaving us with little concrete evidence to substantiate its veracity. One might ponder why the Arab conquerors, who would have been eager to capitalize on selling the coveted metal, would willingly part with such a treasure rather than employ it for their own ambitious purposes.

Even if destiny had granted the Colossus of Rhodes an opportunity to rise anew, its triumph would have likely remained short-lived. Rhodes endured the wrath of numerous seismic upheavals after the cataclysmic tremor of 226 BCE. Moreover, with the advent of Christianity as the dominant force in the region, the inhabitants of Rhodes would have been disinclined to allocate their precious resources toward reconstructing a monument venerating a pagan deity.

Still, the Colossus of Rhodes, an emblem of the island's affluence and influence, became etched within the annals of history. The embellished accounts and descriptions of this architectural marvel rightfully propelled it to secure a coveted position among the illustrious Seven Wonders of the Ancient World.

Summary of Events

- 292–280 BCE: The Colossus of Rhodes, one of the Seven Wonders of the Ancient World, was constructed to represent the sun god Helios in the harbor of Rhodes.

- 228 or 226 BCE: The Colossus of Rhodes fell due to an earthquake.

- c. 225 BCE: Philo of Byzantium became the first recorded historian to mention the Seven Wonders of the Ancient World.

- c. 654 CE: According to Theophanes, a Jewish merchant transported the pieces of the destroyed Colossus of Rhodes to Edessa to be melted down.

Chapter 7 - The Lighthouse of Alexandria

The Lighthouse of Alexandria emerges from the annals of history with an air of majesty and intrigue. Revered as the Pharos of Alexandria, this architectural marvel is said to have graced the island of Pharos, casting its radiant light near the bustling harbor of Alexandria. Imposing in its grandeur, the lighthouse soared to awe-inspiring heights, surpassing over 350 feet (110 meters).

By delving deep into the chronicles of time, we find ourselves transported to the reigns of Ptolemy I and Ptolemy II, which was when this extraordinary beacon first illuminated the Egyptian sky. It was during this same century that the city of Alexandria was envisioned by the conqueror Alexander the Great in the year 331 BCE.

Nestled alongside the gentle flow of the majestic Nile, Alexandria flourished as a hub of trade and commerce. The city boasted not one but two natural harbors, luring merchants from distant lands to its shores. In 305 BCE, under the astute rule of Ptolemy I, Alexandria became the capital of the Ptolemaic dynasty, her influence stretching far and wide across the realm.

And Alexandria's allure extended beyond its economic prowess. A tapestry of cultures walked its vibrant streets, with wanderers and explorers being drawn to the city from every corner of Greece and beyond. In this captivating melting pot of diversity, knowledge, and wisdom, the people found fertile ground to advance the arts, education, and much else.

Alexandria minted its own currency, a testament to its independence and economic prowess. Coins bearing the city's mark served as symbols of trade, unity, and the march of progress. They bore witness to Alexandria's unique place in the tapestry of human civilization.

Today, Alexandria endures as a thriving metropolis, a testament to the resilience of human endeavors. Alexandria claims the honor of being Egypt's second-largest city, with the first being Cairo. The echoes of ancient wonders and the whispers of history permeate the air, inviting all who visit to be swept away by the indomitable allure of this timeless city.

Who Built the Lighthouse of Alexandria?

The construction of the Lighthouse of Alexandria was initiated by Ptolemy I, who reigned from 305 to 282 BCE. Ptolemy is notable for being one of Alexander the Great's generals and the founder of the Ptolemaic dynasty in Egypt. The exact timeline of its construction remains a topic of debate among historians, though. Some sources suggest that the initial construction of the lighthouse occurred around 300 BCE and that its completion took place possibly in 282 or 280 during the reign of Ptolemy II, who governed from 284 to 246 BCE.[6] Alternative theories propose that Ptolemy I commissioned the lighthouse but that the actual construction commenced in 284 and concluded in 246. The primary purpose of this monumental structure was twofold: to facilitate safe navigation for ships approaching the city and to proudly display Alexandria's opulence and grandeur to the world.

Overseeing the construction of the Lighthouse of Alexandria was Sostratus, an esteemed architect hailing from Cnidus, an ancient Greek city situated in Caria, which corresponds to modern-day Turkey. However, some sources say that Sostratus did not design the lighthouse but instead helped to finance the project. The lighthouse once perched atop the limestone islet on the island of Pharos, majestically surveying the bustling port city of Alexandria. This city boasted two distinct harbors, Eunostos and the Megas Limin, both of which benefited from the lighthouse's illuminating presence.

The Lighthouse of Alexandria was dedicated to Zeus, the king of the gods, and possibly the sea god Proteus. Proteus was known for ensuring the safety of seafarers and was revered for his ability to guide ships through

---

[6] You might notice that the regnal years of Ptolemy I and Ptolemy II don't match up. Ptolemy II was declared king by his father in 284 and served as his co-regent.

treacherous waters. Zeus was honored for his unwavering commitment to safeguarding sailors and providing them with direction during their perilous journeys. While it remains challenging to definitively establish whether lighthouses predate the Lighthouse of Alexandria, it still stands as the first recorded lighthouse in human history and the tallest one ever built.[7] After the Lighthouse of Alexandria was built, lighthouses proliferated throughout major Mediterranean cities, serving as beacons of hope for weary travelers and indispensable navigational aids. These towering structures played a pivotal role in identifying perilous reefs and hazardous rocks, offering protection to seafarers traversing the vast expanses of the sea.

A depiction of the Lighthouse of Alexandria (Pharos) by Philip Galle.
https://commons.wikimedia.org/wiki/File:Philip_Galle_-_Lighthouse_of_Alexandria_(Pharos_of_Alexandria)_-_1572.jpg

What Did the Lighthouse of Alexandria Look Like?

The Lighthouse of Alexandria, also known as the pharos, was an iconic structure located on the island of Pharos in Egypt. While the exact details

---

[7] It must be noted that many lists don't count the Lighthouse of Alexandria on lists of the tallest lighthouses since it is possible the numbers were exaggerated.

of its design are uncertain, historians believe that it consisted of three levels with distinct shapes. The first level was rectangular, the second level was octagonal, and the third level was spherical. These unique shapes were intended to set the lighthouse apart from other buildings in the area.

The island was connected to the mainland by a causeway called the Heptastadion, which spanned approximately 4,130 feet (1,260 meters). This causeway played a crucial role in providing access to the island and the lighthouse itself. Accounts by Arab writers suggest that the lighthouse had an interior stairway connecting each floor, as well as an external ramp.

Estimates of the lighthouse's height vary, with a range of 330 to 460 feet. However, the prevailing consensus among historians is that it stood around 350 feet tall, making it the tallest manmade structure of its time and the tallest lighthouse ever built. The lighthouse was constructed using light-colored stone, most likely white, to ensure its visibility as a navigational aid.

The exact lighting system of the lighthouse is a topic of debate. While some ancient sources do not mention the use of light, Pliny the Elder describes a flame in the lighthouse. It is believed that burning oil or papyrus was used to keep the upper part of the tower visible at night. There is uncertainty about whether this lighting system was present from the beginning, though. According to later Arab writers, a polished bronze mirror was used to reflect the flame and enhance its visibility at sea. The mirror could also be utilized to reflect sunlight during the day.

Limited information is available regarding statues or artwork associated with the lighthouse. Depictions on Roman imperial coinage show a tower with a colossal figure and two smaller figures of Triton blowing conch shells, but these depictions do not provide details about the lighthouse's interior or lighting system.

In recent times, underwater explorations have uncovered blocks from a submerged structure in Alexandria's harbor that potentially belong to the legendary lighthouse. However, scholars debate whether these blocks are from the lighthouse itself or from other structures that used repurposed materials.

Overall, while the Lighthouse of Alexandria's precise appearance and features remain elusive, it was an impressive architectural feat and an important symbol of ancient Alexandria.

The Lighthouse of Alexandria's Destruction

Throughout its tumultuous history, the Lighthouse of Alexandria bore the brunt of relentless earthquakes, their destructive force etching scars upon its towering form. The annals of time reveal fleeting glimpses into the specific ravages each earthquake wrought upon this magnificent structure, but comprehensive accounts remain scarce, shrouding the events in mystery. Undoubtedly, the passage of time has led to discrepancies in sources.

The earthquakes that reverberated through Alexandria in the years 796 CE, 951 CE, 956 CE, 1303 CE, and 1323 CE inflicted grave consequences upon the lighthouse. This majestic emblem of the city's opulence and maritime prowess suffered partial collapses and extensive damage.

Nevertheless, the lighthouse continued to shine, as time and time again, engineers and artisans sought to restore and possibly expand the building. They diligently toiled to resurrect the grandeur and functionality of this iconic structure, breathing life into it once more. Such meticulous repairs were undertaken to ensure that the beacon continued to guide and safeguard seafaring vessels navigating the treacherous waters of Alexandria's harbor.

In the annals of the Fatimid period, after the 956 earthquake destroyed part of the lighthouse, a transformative metamorphosis took hold of the structure. Atop its lofty edifice, an imposing dome materialized, an architectural testament to the adaptability and harmonious fusion of Islamic elements within the existing framework. This spiritual transformation endowed the lighthouse with renewed purpose, acting as a union of faith and functionality.

An intriguing linguistic connection unites the architectural design of the lighthouse with the minarets that punctuate the Arab landscape. In the Arabic language, the term for "lighthouse" is *manarah*. This alludes to the influence the lighthouse wielded over the development of minarets.

Yet, following the 14th century CE, the historical accounts abruptly cease talking about the lighthouse. It is widely believed that another cataclysmic earthquake, potentially unfurling its destructive forces in the 1330s CE, eventually sealed the lighthouse's fate. This seismic upheaval likely unleashed unparalleled devastation upon Alexandria.

The granite foundations of the lighthouse found a new purpose in the construction of the resplendent Qaitbay fortress during the 15th century

CE. The fort incorporated the lighthouse's sturdy foundations, turning them into a new bastion of strength.

In the realm of maritime archaeology, explorers of bygone depths have unearthed a trove of fragmented stones and two monumental statues adorning the likeness of Ptolemy I and Queen Berenice, Ptolemy's wife. These precious relics, discovered in close proximity to the lighthouse's remnants, provide tangible evidence of the lighthouse's historical significance and offer a tantalizing glimpse into the past.

The exact number of ships saved by the lighthouse's beacon remains unknown, but it undoubtedly saved many. Alexandria's ancient harbor, a realm of treacherous currents and lurking perils, failed to offer sanctuary to seafarers, as evidenced by the discovery of over forty shipwrecks strewn amidst its depths. The lighthouse likely played a pivotal role in guiding vessels safely into the harbor's protective embrace, though the extent of its impact will never be known.

The Lighthouse of Alexandria bore witness to a tumultuous saga and was beset by unyielding earthquakes and the ravages of time. Yet, despite the scars etched upon its venerable façade, its enduring architectural and cultural legacy reverberates through history. Each restoration, each rebirth, and each lustrous chapter serves as a testament to the profound ingenuity that thrived within the hearts of the ancients, etching the name of the lighthouse in the annals of human achievement.

Summary of Events

- 300-246 BCE: The Lighthouse of Alexandria, one of the Seven Wonders of the Ancient World, is created.

- c. 225 BCE: Philo of Byzantium lists the Seven Wonders of the Ancient World.

- 956 CE: An earthquake caused the partial collapse of the Lighthouse of Alexandria. The top of the lighthouse was later replaced with an Islamic-style dome.

- c. 1330 CE: The Lighthouse of Alexandria finally collapses due to an earthquake.

Conclusion

The Seven Wonders of the Ancient World have captivated individuals for centuries, as they highlight the extraordinary complexity and sheer architectural brilliance that characterized human craftsmanship in antiquity. It is of the utmost importance to emphasize that these legendary lists, which encompass compilations by illustrious figures such as Herodotus, Callimachus of Cyrene, Antipater of Sidon, and Philo of Byzantium, stand as the conventional list that has been passed down through countless generations. Nevertheless, there are other remarkable structures that stand worthy of recognition alongside the wonders on the traditional list.

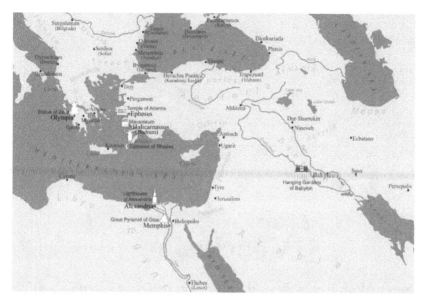

These are the sites of the Seven Wonders of the Ancient World. They were located in Greece, North Africa, and Asia Minor. Construction for these wonders lasted anywhere from 2550 BCE for the Great Pyramid of Giza to potentially 246 BCE for the Lighthouse of Alexandria. The dates for the construction of the wonders vary greatly. The Great Pyramid of Giza is the only ancient wonder on the traditional list that has survived to the present day. However, archaeological digs have uncovered many of the lost wonders of the ancient world, except for the Hanging Gardens of Babylon.

Several ancient lists include the walls of Babylon, an imposing structure that, according to the accounts of Herodotus, spanned a staggering fifty-six miles (ninety kilometers) in length, with select sections being eighty feet (twenty-four kilometers) thick. The wall was 320 feet (97 kilometers) tall! Modern historians think these estimates are exaggerations, but they do help to show how impressive the walls must have been. The walls of Babylon used to be on the traditional lists, but the Lighthouse of Alexandria took their place.

The influence of Christianity impacted later lists created by historians and scholars like Gregory of Tours. His list included sites like Noah's Ark (an ancient wonder on par with the Hanging Gardens of Babylon, for it is not known if it existed or where it was built), Solomon's Temple in Jerusalem, the Grave of the Persian King (it is not known what this refers to, although it is possible it refers to the Mausoleum of Halicarnassus), the Lighthouse of Alexandria, the Colossus of Rhodes, the theater of Heraclea (which was built into a rocky outcrop), and the walls of Babylon.

The Colosseum in Rome, which still stands today, often appears on the lists of ancient wonders, and it is easy to understand why. It was the largest amphitheater ever built and stands right in the center of Rome, making it impossible to miss. It was built of concrete, limestone, and volcanic rock and used to hold the gladiatorial games. It is believed that up to eighty thousand spectators once sat in the Colosseum's seats, watching as bloody battles and plays took place in the arena. The Great Wall of China, a series of walls that cover over thirteen thousand miles (over twenty-one thousand kilometers), and Stonehenge in England are also popular contenders for the list.

Some argue that the list is too focused on the Hellenistic world and that other marvels were created around the world during this time that were just as interesting. Many lists of wonders have been completed in the years, including the Seven Wonders of the New World (which actually includes the Colosseum and the Great Wall of China), the Seven Natural Wonders of the World, and the Seven Wonders of the Solar System, to name a few.

But let's turn back to the traditional list and take one last look at these marvels. The Great Pyramid of Giza still stands as a testament to the grandeur of ancient civilizations. It soared to unimaginable heights, its majestic form cloaked in the resplendent beauty of white limestone, rendering it a breathtaking sight under the sun. Around the pyramids lay the archaeological remnants of the Old Kingdom, unearthing compelling evidence of the rulers' military prowess and the kingdom's profound artistic achievements, further underscoring the legacy of this timeless wonder.

It is not known if the Hanging Gardens of Babylon existed, but its legacy endures all the same. It is exciting to think that the gardens might have once existed, and it is just as exciting diving into the theories about it. If it did exist, it was, no doubt, something truly marvelous to behold.

The resplendent Temple of Artemis in Ephesus claims its rightful place among the seven ancient wonders. Nestled near the tranquil embrace of the sea, this temple exuded an unparalleled allure. Pliny the Elder called it the most mesmerizing structure of the ancient Greek period. Pausanias, the esteemed Greek author of the 2nd century CE, further extolled its magnificence, asserting that it stood unrivaled as the pinnacle of human achievement, a marvel that left the world spellbound.

The inclusion of the Statue of Zeus speaks volumes about its enduring fame and universal recognition. Even before its formal acknowledgment on the list of seven ancient wonders, this grand statue had already etched its presence onto the artistic canvas of civilization, as it was immortalized in vase paintings, gemstones, and coins dating as far back as the 4th century BCE. Coins bearing the likeness of Alexander the Great and Roman Emperor Hadrian (r. 117-138 CE) bore witness to the widespread veneration of the Statue of Zeus, which was adorned with marble replicas of Niobe's offspring upon its regal throne.

The Mausoleum of Halicarnassus, with its colossal proportions and lavish embellishments, found its rightful place among the Seven Wonders of the Ancient World. The esteemed Greek historian Pausanias bestowed upon it the evocative name "Mausolea," an homage to its awe-inspiring size and the masterful sculptures that adorned its resplendent façade. Despite enduring several cataclysmic earthquakes, this imposing mausoleum reportedly remained steadfast until its fateful demise in the 13th century CE.

The Colossus of Rhodes, yet another marvel enshrined on the hallowed list, owed its inclusion to its breathtaking proportions. Originally, the ancient Greeks used the term "colossus" to designate statues of any size, but the construction of the Colossus of Rhodes transformed the word into a symbol of gargantuan magnitude. Sadly, the capricious hand of fate dealt a devastating blow to Rhodes in 228 or 226 BCE when a catastrophic earthquake laid waste to the city and its prized statue. Accounts by the venerable Greek geographer and author Strabo recount the solemn abandonment of the fallen statue, for the Oracle of Delphi foretold dire misfortune should it be reconstructed.

Lastly, the Lighthouse of Alexandria, resplendent in its uniqueness and towering stature, concludes the roster of the Seven Wonders of the Ancient World. Recognized for its distinctive design and soaring height, this remarkable edifice served as a beacon to guide mariners through treacherous waters. Its architectural blueprint, imbued with functional elegance, was emulated in other ancient civilizations, with lighthouses becoming a harbinger of safety and hope for seafarers navigating unfamiliar shores.

The allure of the Seven Wonders of the Ancient World has elicited many emotions and reactions throughout the years, stirring the hearts and minds of countless individuals. These resplendent marvels have served as a profound source of inspiration, compelling humanity to contemplate the magnificence and boundless potential of the human spirit when fueled by creativity, knowledge, and the unyielding determination to construct grand and remarkable structures. Undeniably, these seven wonders stand as a testament to the extraordinary feats of engineering and architectural design achieved by ancient civilizations. As the tides of time continue to shift and new frontiers of exploration unfold, we eagerly anticipate the revelations that await, unlocking the enigmatic wonders of the past with each passing discovery.

Part 2: Seven Wonders of the New World

A Captivating Guide to the Great Wall of China, Colosseum, Petra, Christ the Redeemer, Machu Picchu, Taj Mahal, and Chichén Itzá

Introduction

It was sometime in 450 BCE, and Egypt had just welcomed a special guest. His name was Herodotus, and he hailed from the lands of the Olympian gods: Greece. The man was humble, but he was not merely a traveler. He was a scholar and historian who craved to see the world beyond his borders.

Upon arriving in the lands of the pharaoh, Herodotus was struck with awe the moment he saw the kingdom's architectural splendor. The Greek historian not only recorded wars and political conflicts in his book but was also on the hunt for the world's best sights and structures. And so, upon setting eyes on the Great Pyramids, Herodotus quickly put the descriptions of the colossal structures into words, hoping to share his journey with the world.

The pyramid was not the only structure Herodotus had jotted down in his ancient record. He spent most of his life traveling from one region to another; thus, it is safe to assume his records were filled with descriptions of dozens of impressive architectural wonders he stumbled upon. Perhaps satisfied with the number of wonders he had scribbled down in his journal, Herodotus thought it was time to compile them into one. And so, he journeyed back to the Library of Alexandria, where he would spend hours reading scrolls and writing his latest work.

With the help of Callimachus of Cyrene, Herodotus came up with a list of world wonders that compiled a set of architectural marvels all over the world he had set foot before. The list probably functioned like modern-day travel guides that suggest wondrous destinations to tourists.

Herodotus' list of wonders may have given detailed insight into each magnificent structure and the history behind its construction. Sadly, the list is forever lost to us, as it had long succumbed to the challenging test of time.

Fortunately, a handful of writers during the Middle Ages preserved fragments of his accounts. Through their efforts, we have been granted a precious opportunity to delve into the wonders of antiquity. However, imagination is all we can rely on today; just as his list, all the wonders that impressed Herodotus centuries ago have long vanished, ravaged by wars, natural disasters, or simply the passage of time. Only one endured—the Pyramid of Giza—giving us a small glimpse into the thriving ancient world.

Nevertheless, humanity's unyielding spirit has continually pushed the boundaries of possibility, resulting in the construction of new wonders that captivate our imaginations. Through the ages, new marvels have been brought forth, each with distinctive features and remarkable tales. From an engineering triumph that spans thousands of kilometers of rugged mountains and valleys to a colossal amphitheater and an all-marble mausoleum, these new wonders stand as evidence of the indomitable human spirit and the unrelenting pursuit of greatness. In this context, Herodotus' list found new life; from the Wonders of the Ancient World came a new list called the Seven Wonders of the New World.

Chapter 1 - The Origins and History of the Great Wall of China

Dragons were thought to be mythical creatures that symbolized evil—at least according to most old European beliefs. Though depicted with four legs and a long tail, these dragons also had a pair of large wings that could lift their enormous bodies off the ground, allowing them to travel across the vast skies. They guarded the world's most precious treasures and breathed fire to destroy those who dared to stand in their way—or, perhaps, tried to steal valuables. These fearsome creatures were often categorized as antagonists. The Chinese, however, had a completely different view, believing dragons to be far from malevolent creatures. They were, in fact, symbols of prosperity, good fortune, strength, and protection. Some even claimed they were rulers of the deep sea.

A depiction of a dragon carved onto a tomb.
BabelStone, CC BY-SA 3.0 <https://creativecommons.org/licenses/by-sa/3.0>, via Wikimedia Commons: https://commons.wikimedia.org/wiki/File:Coffin_board_with_dragon_engraving.jpg

Spotting the many differences between the two types of dragons is not a demanding task. Chinese dragons, or "loong," have a pair of horns on top of their heads. Apart from their visible sharp teeth, they also wear beards and whiskers. They do not have wings, but like their Western counterparts, they can fly. Their most prominent characteristic is none other than their body shape: Chinese dragons have a rather long, serpentine body fully covered in scales that are believed to glimmer under the sun, giving them an almost divine appearance.

Depictions of the serpent-like dragon no doubt appear on numerous ancient Chinese artifacts, arts, and literature. However, few know that the Great Wall of China was also a tribute to the mysterious creature. The wall that goes through the natural contours of the landscape is said to resemble the long body of the serpentine dragon sleeping across the land. Whether the legendary wall was intentionally designed to resemble the dragon remains a topic of dispute. However, we can be sure that just as dragons were important in Chinese myths and beliefs, the Great Wall also played a pivotal role in the ancient history of China. This giant structure was an impressive engineering feat that protected the kingdom from dozens of impending dangers for centuries.

Although the Great Wall of China is regarded as one of the wonders of the new world, its construction began many centuries ago—its history goes back to before China was reunited by its very first emperor. Much to the surprise of many, the Great Wall was initially not a single set of walls; instead, it began with a series of walls constructed during China's Warring States period.

Like the ancient Egyptians, Greeks, and even the Japanese, the Chinese went through a long period of divided kingdoms. Believed to have begun in 475 BCE, the Warring States period was when the different states of ancient China fought against one another, each vying for control, territory, and resources. Great battles, strategic alliances, and vicious betrayals were common during this point of time. New military tactics and defense strategies were continuously developed throughout these years.

Parts of the Great Wall originating from the Ming Dynasty.

Severin.stalder, CC BY-SA 3.0 <https://creativecommons.org/licenses/by-sa/3.0>, via Wikimedia Commons:
https://commons.wikimedia.org/wiki/File:The_Great_Wall_of_China_at_Jinshanling-edit.jpg

The ancient Chinese were always renowned for their exceptional skills in building fortified walls. With the growing turmoil at the time of the divided kingdoms, having their territories heavily protected by defensive walls was deemed crucial, especially for the most notable contenders of the war: the states of Qin, Zhao, Wei, Yan, and Ming. These walls were used to defend themselves from each other and hold off any attacks by the nomadic raiders of the north.

The Great Walls of the Warring States

The state of Wei began as a small entity in the seventh century, but it grew tremendously over the centuries through strategic alliances and military conquests. By 403 BCE, Wei had become one of the leading states during the Warring States period. Though Wei often faced threats imposed by the nomadic tribes of the north, the state was also plagued by frequent conflicts with its neighboring state, Qin. And so, to resist attacks and protect its people from the powerful Qin, Wei began constructing its own fortified walls in 358 BCE. Made out of rammed earth and further reinforced by wooden beams, stones, and bricks, the Great Wall of Wei stretched along the Yellow River for over three hundred kilometers, bordering its greatest nemesis, the Qin state, on the west. Though the climate was harsh and the terrains were rough—the steep mountains had claimed the lives of many laborers—the construction was completed in just seven years.

Garrisons were placed along the wall, and watchtowers were installed to spot enemies from a distance. Despite successfully repelling daring enemies who wished to lay it waste, Wei eventually suffered a terrible loss when the forces of Qin rose to their ultimate power.

The state of Yan also had its own sets of walls to barricade its people from the dangers of the war. However, the construction of the walls was only launched after the state's successful campaign against the Donghu people. Under the reign of King Zhao of Yan, the formidable general Qin Kai is said to have defeated the nomadic tribe, clearing the way for the state to conquer the Liaodong Peninsula. Beginning at the recently-conquered Liaodong Peninsula, the Great Wall of Yan stretched into Chifeng and ran through the northern region of Hebei. Parts of the southern walls were then further fortified as a defense against the state of Zhao—which, like the rest of the warring states, had also secured its territories by erecting a series of fortified walls.

The most impressive of all was, of course, the walls constructed by Qin. Once a peripheral state with little influence in the Chinese political sphere, Qin transformed when reforms were introduced by a man named Shang Yang, who became the state's chief advisor. Through his reforms, the state's government was successfully centralized, and its military forces grew into a formidable power. Yang led his soldiers against the Wei and drove them out of the comfort of their fortified city. Years later, the Qin also obliterated the state of Yiqu (located northwest of Qin), leaving it with no choice but to submit. This, however, was only the beginning of Qin's aggressive expansion. In 221 BCE, under the reign of King Zheng, the Warring States period finally ended when Qin came out on top after having conquered the rest of the individual states.

Emperor Qin Shi Huang and His Great Wall: The Precursor to the Current Great Wall of China

King Zheng, later known as Qin Shi Huang (or Shi Huangdi) was the first emperor of unified China and the founder of the Qin dynasty. Historians, however, have mixed views of the autocratic emperor. Some considered him a hero for ending the centuries-long war and uniting China, while others claim he was an absolute brutal ruler whose obsessions were only power and immortality. (He was the famed emperor who launched several quests in search of immortality and was interred with thousands of Terracotta Army when he finally met his end.)

Nevertheless, Qin Shi Huang was also the emperor who gave birth to the foundation of the Great Wall of China, which greatly protected the kingdom from harm.

Although the kingdom's east and west were protected by natural barriers—the Pacific Ocean and the Tibetan Plateau, respectively—its northern territories were exposed, making them highly vulnerable to the barbaric nomads who had long attempted to invade the Chinese lands and secure its agricultural wealth. And so, when the emperor noticed the increasing power of the nomadic Xiongnu, he dispatched 300,000 of his army against them without hesitation. Under the command of Meng Tian, the Qin army successfully drove the Xiongnu further northward, thus reversing their ambitious expansion plans. Not risking any more invasions from the north, the emperor laid out his grand plans to construct a single set of fortified walls known as the "Wan-Li Chang Cheng" or the "10,000-li Long Wall." Spearheaded by Meng Tian, the construction began, which connected some of the walls left by the former warring states.

Given how tremendous the project was, an unimaginable number of laborers were needed. Soldiers and commoners were enlisted to work on the walls. Hundreds of thousands of peasants and sentenced criminals were also conscripted to ensure the project's completion. Once chosen to lend their hands on the walls, the majority were not allowed to deny the work; they were guaranteed a sword to their necks should they defy their emperor. The construction was harsh, as the laborers were said to have been forced to work on the rammed earth and rocks collected from the mountainous ranges with only a short amount of rest. Many perished with tools still held firmly in their hands due to the merciless climate, exhaustion, and extreme dehydration. The bodies of the poor builders were either interred within the walls or in grave pits nearby. Despite the brutal construction process, the emperor's defense system was realized; upon completion, the wall spanned from Lintao in the west and into Liaodong in the east.

The fall of the Qin dynasty resulted in the disrepair of the wall, but the Han dynasty rulers soon restored it. The walls were repaired to their most glorious state, expanded, and greatly fortified with more watch towers. Under the Han, the Great Wall reached nearly 6,000 kilometers, covering the regions of Dunhuang to the Bohai Sea. The construction work on the walls during this period was no different than during the Qin dynasty; under the reign of Emperor Han-Wudi, forced labor continued, and the wall's reputation as the worst place of suffering spread beyond the empire's frontiers.

However, given the extreme length of the walls, the Chinese emperors were often plagued with a headache: constantly maintaining such a monumental structure would be unimaginably costly. Thus, the Great Wall fell into disrepair once again. However, in the 1200s, one particular force would recognize the wall's disuse as an opportunity to exploit it to their advantage.

At first, China flourished under the glorious reign of the Song dynasty. Scholars today often admire the Song economic revolution, as this was the period when China's agriculture, ironworking, and printing technologies grew tremendously. The dynasty also saw growth in the state's population, allowing the cities to thrive and transform into hubs of various activities. Unfortunately, as prosperous as the dynasty was, it was also forced to deal with the growing danger posed by its northern rivals: the ferocious Mongol warriors under the legendary reign of Genghis Khan. Under Khan, the Mongols formed a well-organized and exceptionally formidable army capable of overthrowing any forces—including the Chinese empire.

In 1211, the Mongols rode to the Juyongguan Pass and breached the Great Wall, destroying its reputation as the world's most impregnable fortification. Bribing the Chinese officials and guards, the cunning forces of Genghis Khan managed to penetrate the walls several more times until they eventually besieged the capital of Yanjing (known today as Beijing) in 1215. Though the city was plundered heavily, the Mongols never intended to sack it entirely. It was only in 1279 that the Mongols, under the leadership of Kublai Khan (the grandson of Genghis), successfully overthrew the Song dynasty. With their grand victory, Kublai Khan established the Yuan dynasty, which ruled over China for a century.

Under the Yuan dynasty, China faced no resistance from the north, which led the Great Wall into further disrepair. The structure was only refortified when the Chinese regained control over their empire. In 1368, the Mongols were defeated, and China was finally under the control of local emperors from the Ming dynasty. Learning from their past mistakes, the emperors reinforced the Great Wall using sturdier materials, such as modern bricks, stones, and mortar.

Watchtowers were also erected every three to five hundred meters along the walls—when enemies were spotted, guards on the watchtowers would signal for reinforcements using smoke, gunpowder, and flags. Towering over seven meters high with an impressive width of five to seven meters, the Ming Great Wall could accommodate either ten armed soldiers standing shoulder-to-shoulder or five cavalrymen in formation side-by-side. Along the walls, one could spot two types of openings: smaller ones created especially for the archers and bigger holes used to drop heavy rocks on advancing invaders.

View of the Great Wall from a watchtower.

The refortification project spanned a century and undoubtedly required immense labor and resources. Though much of the Great Wall succumbed to the test of time, many of its sections still stand tall today. In fact, it is the Ming Great Wall we often see as a backdrop for tourists visiting China.

However, the walls did not protect China for long, as the Chinese were, yet again, left with no choice but to bow down to the power they intended to repel. Noticing the chaos brewing in the capital of Beijing, the Manchurians quickly took action. They successfully overthrew the Ming and established the Qing dynasty, which later incorporated the Mongols. Under the Qing, China's territory expanded far into Mongolia and beyond the Great Wall. And so, the walls fell into disuse once again, and the structure eroded over time. The sturdy bricks and stones were plundered and used as building materials for other constructions. Nevertheless, parts of the walls served as a defense system one last time during World War II when the Chinese faced a possible invasion from the Japanese.

The Great Wall of China in 1907.
https://commons.wikimedia.org/wiki/File:Greatwall_large.jpg

Today, the fate of the Great Wall is somewhat ironic. Once built to keep invaders out of China, it now welcomes thousands of foreign visitors every year. While the original purpose of the Great Wall may be long gone, mentions of the structure will never disappear from our history books. The Great Wall of China has survived countless centuries of war, natural disasters, and neglect, yet parts of it still stand strong, providing us with a vivid image of the remarkable achievements of ancient China.

Chapter 2 - The Legend of Meng Jiangnü: The Woman Who Tore Down the Great Wall

The myth of Meng Jiangnü occurred sometime between 221 and 206 BCE when the Chinese kingdom was under the control of the emperor Qin Shi Huang. At the time, agriculture was the mainstay of the economy and the foundation of society. While the nobles and aristocrats enjoyed a privileged lifestyle flooded with abundant wealth, power, and prestige, the commoners belonged at the bottom of the hierarchy and order. Indeed, those at the top of the social pyramid had dwellings within the fortified city, each adorned with fine arts, sculptures, and furniture. However, the same could not be said of the less fortunate ones that made up the majority of the kingdom's population. These people could not afford to enjoy a life behind the safe walls of big cities, so they built their houses on the outskirts, with farming as their main source of income.

Far to the southern part of the kingdom lived a couple who went by the surname of Meng. They led nothing but a simple life. They would rise when the sun emerged on the horizon, and probably well-rested from their sleep the night before, the couple would begin working on their farm. Though their routine was the same every day, the Mengs found great joy and satisfaction in their work, taking pride in the small victories of each harvest and the humble pleasures of their lives.

One morning, as the Mengs tended to their farm, they found a small packet of bottle gourd seeds. Without expecting anything peculiar to happen, they planted the seeds in the rich soil of their yard. As the days passed, the bottle gourd vines grew with surprising vigor, twining their way around the walls of the Mengs' humble dwelling and creeping into the yard of their neighbors, the Jiangs. At first, the Mengs worried that the vines might be seen as an unwelcome intrusion. But to their surprise, the old couple welcomed them with open arms, eagerly tending to the growing crop alongside the Mengs. Thus began a warm and enduring friendship between the two families, marked by the simple pleasures of tending the vine and the shared joys of their daily lives.

As the days grew shorter and the leaves turned golden, the plant finally bore fruit and was ready to be harvested. Eagerly, the two couples gathered around the plant, marveling at the size and shape of the gourd that hung from its vines. With great care, they plucked it from the vine. Since they both took care of the plant equally, they decided to cut the gourd in half and share it with each other. To their surprise, what they found inside was like nothing they had ever seen.

A tiny, innocent infant lay curled within the gourd. The Meng and Jiang families watched as the infant opened her eyes as if she had just awakened from a deep slumber. It was indeed a peculiar event, but the two couples had no time to ponder about logic; instead, they were thinking of who would raise the child. Since both couples had no children, the two families decided to adopt the infant and raise her as their daughter. Combining their surnames, they named the girl Meng Jiangnü—a name that would soon echo throughout the kingdom.

Despite their modest lives, the two families blessed Meng Jiangnü with the most tender love and boundless care. Though they achieved only small victories from their harvests each season, the Mengs and Jiangs never failed to feed their beloved daughter to the fullest and made her contentment their top priority. In gratitude for their absolute care, Meng Jiangnü assisted with the household chores—she did so willingly and without a single complaint crossing her mind. Days turned into years, and Meng Jiangnü soon turned into a young, beautiful woman whose remarkable character and admirable qualities won the hearts of many.

Meng Jiangnü was said to have loved spending her leisure time strolling around gardens and parks, marveling at mother nature's beauty. On one fine evening, as she was walking through a tranquil garden, Meng Jiangnü was startled by sudden rustling sounds from nearby bushes. Curious, she slowly approached the bushes to investigate the sound. Halfway towards where the bushes were, Meng Jiangnü froze the moment she saw a figure of a man hiding among the bushes—who, at the same time, was peering at her every move. Frightened, Meng Jiangnü began running away, with other sources claiming she went to fetch her parents.

Perhaps feeling guilty of unintentionally scaring her, the man quickly emerged from hiding while calling out to the fleeing Meng Jiangnü, asking her to stop. Dressed in tattered clothes, with a rugged look on his bare face, the man introduced himself as Fan Xiliang and reassured her that he meant no harm. Despite her initial fright, Meng Jiangnü noticed the sense of desperation in Fan Xiliang's shaky voice. And so, she decided to lend her ears to the mysterious man.

In an anxious tone, Fan Xiliang told Meng Jiangnü the real reason behind his hiding: he did not do so to stalk her but to avoid getting caught by the government officials actively conscripting men to work on the Great Wall. He added that he had been on the run for days and had not touched a single meal since leaving home. As Fan Xiliang explained his backstory, Meng Jiangnü grew to sympathize with his situation. She had also noticed something else as she listened to his story: beneath his desperate and rugged look, Fan Xiliang was a handsome young man whose gentle manner would attract anyone.

Without hesitation, Meng Jiangnü knew she must help Fan Xiliang. And so, she took the young man home and introduced him to her parents. Just over a short period, Meng Jiangnü and Fan Xiliang bonded as if they had known each other for years. They talked until they forgot the existence of time and laughed at each other's jokes until their worries disappeared—at least for a little while. Eventually, the two fell deeply in love and could not see a future without one another.

The story of Meng Jiangnü and Fan Xiliang's marriage has been told and retold in various versions throughout history. One version suggests Meng Jiangnü first expressed her desire to marry Fan Xiliang. She had seen his charming qualities and how gentle he was with her, and she immediately told her parents of her wish. Seeing how happy their daughter was with Fan Xiliang, the Mengs and the Jiangs agreed to marry them off without hesitation.

However, another source provides a slightly different perspective. According to this version, Fan Xiliang initially rejected Meng Jiangnü's marriage proposal. He was worried that she could be pulled into his troubles should she become his wife. Despite Xiliang's reservations, Meng Jiangnü was persistent and firmly stated that she would marry no one except him. Her unwavering love and determination eventually won him over; Fan Xiliang, who deep down could not bear losing her, agreed to marry her.

The two were married in a simple yet heartfelt celebration, perhaps with only a modest feast accompanied by a small group of close friends and neighbors. Despite their humble circumstances, their love for each other was strong, and they were filled with hope and optimism for their future. However, the world was not filled with only rainbows and sunshine. Unbeknownst to the newlyweds, their time together was shortened from forever to only three days.

An envious stranger had just learned the story of Fan Xiliang's initial hiding. Though details about the stranger are minimal, old writings suggest he had been in love with Meng Jiangnü. Though the love was only one-sided, he could not bear seeing her with another man. And so, out of jealousy, the man reported Fan Xiliang's whereabouts to the government officials.

As soon as the authorities received word, they wasted no time tracking down Fan Xiliang. Despite his clear protests and the pleas of Meng Jiangnü, who begged the officials for mercy, Fan Xiliang was dragged away and immediately taken to the construction site of the Great Wall. He had to leave behind the life he had dreamed of with Meng Jiangnü and accept a fate that many dreaded: to work day and night without rest on the wall until the construction was completed or he breathed his last breath.

The news of Fan Xiliang's arrest and forced labor on the Great Wall spread quickly throughout the small village, leaving Meng Jiangnü devastated and beyond heartbroken. She had just begun building a life, but without Fan Xiliang by her side, their home felt empty and devoid of warmth. Instead of spending her free time wandering around gardens and surrounding herself with nature, Meng Jiangnü stayed indoors. She spent endless hours gazing at the stars, praying for a miracle, and hoping for a way to reunite with her beloved husband.

A year passed, and Meng Jiangnü never heard anything from her husband. She was constantly plagued with nightmares each night, with the recurring dream of Fan Xiliang dressed in thin clothing, shivering terribly as he moved one brick after another in the heavy winter snow. Longing for her husband and worried about his state on the construction site, Meng Jiangnü grew determined to find a way to hold Fan Xiliang in her arms again. And so, her routine changed one day: she began filling her autumn hours with knitting clothes, each padded with cotton to keep her husband warm. Knitting kept her occupied all day and eventually filled her eyes with the hope of finally reuniting with Fan Xiliang again.

Nevertheless, Meng Jiangnü knew that finding her husband at the Great Wall was no easy task. She had heard rumors of the harsh conditions and the many deaths during the wall's construction. But the rumors did not stop her from continuing her mission. She asked around and gathered information on how to reach the site. Finally, she set off on a long and treacherous journey, traveling only by foot and relying on the kindness of strangers to get her closer to her destination—and, soon, closer to the gentle touch of her dear husband.

After months, she finally arrived at the foot of the Great Wall, which lay on the present Shanhaiguan Pass. There, Meng Jiangnü was met with the sight of endless lines of workers exposed to the harsh temperature of winter, each carrying heavy bricks to arrange on the Great Wall. With haste, Meng Jiangnü searched among the workers, calling out Fan Xiliang's name over and over again. Her voice echoed through the walls, but there was no answer, let alone a response from a voice she longed for. Her voice grew hoarse as she desperately called out her husband's name.

Meng Jiangnü only stopped calling when she noticed a man approaching her. Also a forced laborer, the man claimed to have known her husband. Unfortunately, the next few words that came out of his mouth broke Meng Jiangnü's heart into a thousand pieces. He informed her that Fan Xiliang had died some time ago, and his body had been interred within the walls like hundreds of others who succumbed to the same end. Noticing that Meng Jiangnü had turned frozen from the news, the man offered to lead her toward the spot where her husband had been buried.

Only after arriving at the section of the wall where Fan Xiliang had been interred and left to rot was Meng Jiangnü able to express her feelings. She wept continuously, and some claim her tears fell down her cheeks non-stop for three consecutive nights. On her last day of weeping, the sky turned black, and a fierce wind began to blow, though no rain ever touched the ground. Instead, her weeping had invited chaos; in the blink of an eye, a section of the wall that measured at least four hundred kilometers long crumbled to the earth's surface, exposing many human remains buried under the wall.

Nevertheless, Meng Jiangnü could not identify Fan Xiliang's remains. And so, she prayed to the gods for a way to recognize her husband one last time. She then bit her finger until her blood ran down her arm. She let a drop of her blood touch each corpse and skeleton on the ground along the ruins of the wall. It was said that the blood would only dissolve when it touched Fan Xiliang's remains, and that was how Meng Jiangnü finally identified her husband. The moment she saw the blood dissolve, her heart was filled with relief and sorrow. Indeed, she had found her husband, but he was gone forever.

An illustration of Meng Jiangnü weeping by the Great Wall.
https://commons.wikimedia.org/wiki/File:Meng_Jiang_Nu_Song_Dynasty_Lie_Nu_Zhuan.jpg

The story of Meng Jiangnü did not end there. At the time of her arrival at the construction site, Emperor Qin Shi Huang was also nearby to tour the progress of the Great Wall. And so, when a section of the wall collapsed, word traveled fast enough that the emperor managed to confront Meng Jiangnü before she could depart with her husband's remains. The emperor was popular for his cruelty; thus, it was no surprise when he immediately punished the person responsible for the collapse.

However, upon laying eyes on the devastated young woman, the emperor immediately grew fond of Meng Jiangnü and wished to marry her. Meng Jiangnü knew defying the emperor would never end well, so she had no choice but to agree. But she had no plans on making the marriage easy. She proposed three conditions to the emperor before they could wed. First, her deceased husband must be given not only a proper funeral but also a grand one. Second, the Chinese court, including the emperor himself, must mourn Fan Xiliang's terrible fate. Third and last, Meng Jiangnü wished to visit the sea.

Of course, the emperor was not entirely happy when Meng Jiangnü requested to honor her dead husband; after all, he was but a commoner whose name he did not know. But he was headstrong on marrying her, so the emperor agreed to all three conditions.

When the funeral was done, and Fan Xiliang's remains were finally put to rest, Meng Jiangnü moved on to her next plan. No force on earth could make her marry the man responsible for her husband's demise. And so, when the emperor fulfilled her third condition, Meng Jiangnü jumped into the Bohai Sea, drowning herself, hoping she would be reunited with Fan Xiliang in another life.

The legend of Meng Jiangnü is a powerful reminder of the harsh reality faced by countless peasants who worked on the construction of the Great Wall. Although the tale blurs the lines between fact and fiction, it is rooted in historical truth. The legend offers a vivid glimpse into the struggle of those who worked tirelessly to build one of the world's greatest wonders and serves as a reminder that behind every great work of history lies a complex and often tragic human story.

Chapter 3 - The Colosseum: Rome's Most Popular Wonder in Its Glory Days

It was the 18th of July in 64 CE, and the Romans were about to welcome a tragedy into their city unwillingly. The first few signs could be seen in the merchant shops close to the Circus Maximus, Rome's famed chariot-racing stadium. Huge clouds of smoke began to form in the air, followed by screams of terror echoing from one corner to the other. Soon, high winds came, spreading terror to the northern districts. The citizens' slumber was disrupted, and they all burst through their doors, hoping to escape from death and catch a whiff of fresh air once again. Many, however, failed, falling lifeless on the ground with their flesh burnt to a crisp. Houses became ashes in a split second, Romans resorted to looting and violence, parents lost their children, and the poor lost faith in living. While hundreds were engulfed in the blazing fire, those given mercy by the angry ancient gods were spared, though they had nothing left. They were left homeless, without a coin in their coffers. This was one of Rome's greatest tragedies—a merciless incident that took the life of many and destroyed over half of the Eternal City. This was the Great Fire of Rome.

A depiction of the Great Fire of Rome.
https://commons.wikimedia.org/wiki/File:Robert,_Hubert_-_Incendie_%C3%A0_Rome_-.jpg

Where was Nero, the reigning emperor, when the great chaos took over his city? the Romans might have angrily wondered. Some said he was aware of the fire devouring his city but had made himself comfortable and was playing music behind the safe walls of his villa far from Rome. Others claimed he was the one who instigated the fire. Whether these accusations should be considered remains a dispute. However, none could deny that his actions following the tragedy caused his subjects, especially the aristocrats, to despise him terribly.

As the fifth Roman emperor and the last of the Julio-Claudian dynasty, Nero undoubtedly had big shoes to fill. The commoners initially favored him, and he showed signs of being a great ruler during the early years of his reign. It was only after his mother's death, according to ancient sources, that Nero began to unleash his tyrannical acts. The emperor knew he must act, so he opened the doors of his palace for his subjects to take shelter and prevented starvation by providing food supplies paid for from his own treasury. Nevertheless, the accusations soon reached his ears. Realizing he needed a scapegoat, Nero blamed the Christians and led the first Christian persecution. They were severely tortured and executed in public. Though houses were rebuilt and restoration projects for the city were launched, Nero also had something else in mind.

The emperor focused more on building the Golden House, a sumptuous palace for himself where he planned on hosting wild parties and lavish banquets. To fund the work needed to realize his dreams, Nero abused his power. He imposed high taxes on his people, seized lands owned by the aristocrats, imposed heavier tributes on the empire's provinces, and devalued the Roman currency. This, however, was the last straw. Conspiracies and rebellions began to occur the following year. Nero was announced public enemy and lost the support of everyone around him, resulting in his suicide in 68 CE.

Though Rome applauded upon hearing news of Nero's death, the empire was far from steady. It was ruled by several incompetent rulers (each ruling only for months) until Vespasian finally took the mantle in December 69 CE. The Flavian emperor planned to erase the traces Nero and his failed successors had left all over Rome, so he gave the land once taken by the dead emperor back to the Romans. To please the Roman citizens, Vespasian made a symbolic gesture; he passed a decree that a grand amphitheater would be built on the site of Nero's Golden House. Here, his people could enjoy nearly endless gladiatorial games and other performances.

The grand project took place sometime in 70-72 CE and would be completed almost a decade later. However, Vespasian never lived long enough to witness the completion of the grand amphitheater; the emperor is believed to have fallen ill and died in 79 CE. His eldest son and successor, Titus, continued his father's ambition and oversaw the construction project to its completion. Initially known to the ancient Romans as the Flavian Amphitheatre, the structure is known today as the Colosseum.

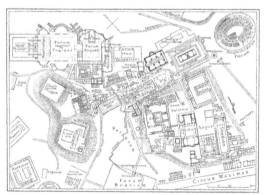

A map showing the Colosseum (top right corner).

Many had been waiting for the completion of the grand amphitheater. Seeing how intrigued his subjects were once they laid eyes on the final design of the Colosseum, Titus thought it would be fitting to hold a grand opening ceremony. The inauguration of the Colosseum took place in 80 CE, and it was indeed one of the most unforgettable events in the history of ancient Rome.

Ancient records state that the ceremony began with an elaborate procession of the emperor, who was fully adorned in his purple imperial regalia. Titus was also accompanied by senators, high-ranking officials, and members of the Roman elite, each showcasing their wealth and nobility through their garments.

A series of shows were organized to keep the citizens entertained. Titus had also announced a hundred days of gladiatorial games to commemorate the structure's completion. Venationes, or animal hunts, were also held; spectators would cheer in unison whenever the gladiators successfully slaughtered a beast. Apart from vicious fights and bloodied warriors, the opening of the Colosseum also included theatrical performances and music shows.

A depiction of the Colosseum minted on a coin dated from 80 CE.

Just as anyone would have expected, the works on such a colossal amphitheater required extensive planning and engineering, especially since the structure was built on a site that was once an artificial lake within Nero's lavish garden. To commence construction, the Romans must first drain the lake. And so, they dug out a series of drains nearly eight meters beneath the ground to draw the water away from the site. Only then would they construct the foundation. To prevent the giant elliptical-shaped structure from collapsing, concrete foundations were carefully constructed deep underground. Apart from the popular Roman concrete, the Colosseum was also made of travertine stone, easily quarried from the ancient town of Albulae. The only problem was that the town was over thirty kilometers from Rome. So, the Romans constructed a road to ease the transportation of the travertine stones. Historians claim that over this newly-constructed road, the Romans (or their slaves) could move at least 240,000 carts daily.

Today, the overall shape of the Colosseum might appear circular and rather simple to some, but the structure has gone through countless episodes of destruction throughout the years. In its glory days, the Colosseum was considered one of the most complex structures ever built by human hands. The unnamed architects behind the wondrous structure carefully used extremely detailed mathematical calculations to shape every inch of the arches, vaults, and even the spectators' seats.

Upon completion, the Colosseum measured 188 meters long and 156 meters wide. The structure towered fifty-seven meters above ground and was divided into four stories. Within the Colosseum itself was not one but several centers. Impressively, the width of the auditorium and arena was the same as the structure's entire height. The amphitheater also featured eighty entrance arches; each measured exactly twenty Roman feet wide (equivalent to nearly six meters) and was built less than a meter apart. These arches were crucial to allowing a smooth flow of spectators to enter and exit the amphitheater. The arena itself had wooden floors, though they were covered by sand. To protect the cheering spectators from the burning sun, parts of the Colosseum were covered with canvas.

Ancient writings stated that the Colosseum could accommodate up to 50,000 people at once. While the gladiators and caged wild animals were placed in the hypogeum beneath the arena before the fights began, the spectators were seated according to their social classes. The more privileged the citizen was, the closer their seat to the arena. Unsurprisingly, the top tier, which provided the best view, was granted to the emperor.

Those of the Roman courts and social elites were given seats on the highest tier, lower only than the emperor's box. The second tier was reserved for government officials and wealthy businessmen, while seating on the third tier was for ordinary Roman citizens. Women, the poor, and slaves, on the other hand, sat only on wooden benches on the lowest ground with limited views.

The remnants of the tiered seating.
Sean MacEntee from Monaghan, Ireland, CC BY 2.0
<https://creativecommons.org/licenses/by/2.0>, via Wikimedia Commons:
https://commons.wikimedia.org/wiki/File:The_Colosseum_(9554989427).jpg

Gladiatorial games were indeed the Romans' favorite type of entertainment. The Colosseum would be swarmed by tens of thousands of citizens whenever an emperor decided to host a game—usually to celebrate a triumph. However, the Colosseum was not just used for gladiatorial fights and mock naval battles; priests also used the amphitheater to conduct religious ceremonies—typically done before the start of a gladiatorial games. When there was supposed to be a sacrificial ceremony, the Romans would install a marble altar in the middle of the arena. Whether it was done as a dedication to Diana, Jupiter, or even Mars, it was common for the ceremony to include animal sacrifice. The sex of the sacrificial animal must correspond to the sex of the gods they were honoring. Sources also suggest that even the colors of the animals varied: white animals were sacrificed only in the name of the gods residing in the upper celestial world, while black ones were reserved for gods of the underworld.

The Colosseum arena, showing the hypogeum.

Though the Colosseum was an important structure in the Roman world, it would soon witness its slow abandonment. The spread of Christianity in Rome played a vital role in disusing the glorious amphitheater. As more Romans openly embraced Christianity, they began to deem gladiatorial contests as a form of entertainment that was opposite their beliefs. The fights were also heavily intertwined with Roman paganism; hence, it would be fitting that they were stopped. And so, the popularity of gladiatorial contests declined when Rome entered the fifth century CE. Eventually, the shows disappeared.

Without the gladiatorial fights, the Colosseum plunged into a period of disuse. The structure was then forced to endure several natural disasters resulting in its damage (though the amphitheater already appeared mutilated due to the Romans' constant harvest of its marble, used in constructing other buildings). A major earthquake then hit the Colosseum sometime in 443 CE, but it was the one in 1349 CE that severely damaged the structure. The Colosseum lost a huge chunk of its southern wall, ruining its perfect elliptical shape. The appearance of the Colosseum we see today resulted from this earthquake.

The Colosseum today.

Restoring such major damage would cost the empire a fortune. Sadly, the empire was on the verge of collapse: the Romans were crippled with political challenges and economic and financial disasters. When the Western Roman Empire fell into the hands of the Germanic barbarian tribes, the once magnificent Colosseum fell into complete neglect and abandonment.

Although the Colosseum no longer holds shows and performances, and its facade is permanently damaged, the amphitheater remains a symbol of ancient Roman engineering and culture. Its architectural design and intriguing history never fail to captivate visitors. Indeed, the structure was heavily neglected in ancient times. But today, efforts have been exhausted to preserve and restore it so that it will last for centuries to come. In the modern world, the Colosseum no longer serves as a site of vicious fights or sacrificial rituals; instead, it stands as evidence of the remarkable achievements of ancient Rome and its enduring legacy in architectural history.

Chapter 4 - From Sand to Sea: Gladiatorial Combat and Naval Reenactments at the Colosseum

It was a day unlike any other in Rome. The nobles had left the comfort of their domus (a type of Roman house owned by the rich), the farmers had hung their sickles earlier than usual, and even the slaves had earned their rest just for today. It was a day when a grand gladiatorial game would soon take place under the massive sponsorship of the reigning emperor.

As the sun reached its zenith, the amphitheater was already filled to the brim. Thousands of spectators had taken their seats, with the wealthy given the best of views, while slaves and women occupied the lowest seats where their views were often restricted. Unlike in a modern theater where the air is quiet, the Roman amphitheater was the opposite. Amidst the grand arches and towering walls, the spectators let out a series of voices and cheers that blended into a deafening roar, sounds that clearly expressed their excitement for the game to begin.

The atmosphere grew even more restless when trumpets were blared, announcing the arrival of the emperor, fully adorned with a wreath on his head and a purple toga hugging his old yet stiff figure. With his arrival came the commencement of the gladiatorial games, which resulted in a round of unsynchronized applause and cheers from the thousands of spectators. Then, the gates at the far end of the arena were cracked open, followed by the sounds of clashing armor and heavy weapons dragged through the dry sand.

The cheers continued as the Romans saw two gladiators stepping out of the wooden gates. One was taller and bigger than the other, though each had a formidable figure. Their bodies had been covered in oil, highlighting their muscular frames from years of hardcore training.

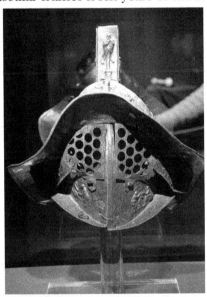

A gladiator helmet found in Pompeii.
Carole Raddato from FRANKFURT, Germany, CC BY-SA 2.0
<https://creativecommons.org/licenses/by-sa/2.0>, via Wikimedia Commons:
https://commons.wikimedia.org/wiki/File:Gladiator_helmet_found_in_Pompeii_and_richly_decora
ted_with_scenes_of_Greek_mythology,_Gladiators_%E2%80%93_Death_and_Triumph_at_the_C
olosseum_exhibition,_Museum_und_Park_Kalkriese_(9618142634).jpg

The taller one was equipped with a gladius (a short sword best for quick slashes) and a shield, while the other wielded a long trident. When it was time to fight, the two vicious gladiators circled each other, their eyes locked in a deadly stare—perhaps to find each other's vulnerabilities. This was the moment the amphitheater went silent as the crowd held their breath, waiting for the first strike. After a few moments of observation, the gladiator with the trident used his agility and lunged forward, hoping he could at least thrust his godly weapon into his opponent's thigh. The other gladiator, however, was popular for his quick reflexes; he managed to dodge the attack.

Then, the crowds erupted in anticipation, each bellowing their support of their chosen champion—some even placed bets on which gladiator would fall on that day. The next few moments were filled with metal ringing against metal and armor clattering as the gladiators parried, dodged, and counterattacked their opponent. Whenever there was a successful attack and a splatter of blood touched the ground, the spectators let aloud gasps or cheers.

It did not take long for the clean and oiled torsos of the gladiators to be marked with bloody cuts and bruises. Yet, they continued to fight with unyielding determination, hoping to see the light of day again tomorrow. With every blow, the cheers grew louder, accompanied by groans and applause.

The finale came when one gladiator successfully seized an opportunity he had been calculating since the fight started. His opponent might have had a bigger figure, allowing him to attack with force, but his weight had tired him too fast. And so, without hesitation, the one armed with a trident quickly disarmed his opponent, sending his sword spiraling through the air, followed by a strike in the legs. The unarmed gladiator fell to his knees. The crowd erupted in a collective gasp, their excitement reaching a fever pitch.

A depiction of a gladiatorial fight.
https://commons.wikimedia.org/wiki/File;Jean-Leon_Gerome_Pollice_Verso.jpg

Although already considered victorious, the gladiator had one last choice: he must determine whether to let his opponent survive another day, despite them being friends before they were forcefully brought to the arena. He held his trident high, his posture poised to deliver the final blow. However, instead of delivering the death blow, the victorious gladiator extended his hand, offering mercy to his opponent. The spectators erupted into loud applause combined with shouts of admiration for his actions. Though many enjoyed the finale, some were dissatisfied, as if not enough blood was spilled.

Gladiatorial fights were not always popular in ancient Rome. While certain scholars believe that gladiatorial games were borrowed from the Etruscans, who usually held them in honor of their gods, others claim that the Roman games did not merely serve as entertainment but as rituals in funeral ceremonies. However, over time, these games grew in popularity and eventually became a form of public entertainment typically held ten to twelve times a year. Before the construction of the Colosseum, gladiatorial games were held in various venues across ancient Rome. Not limited to only amphitheaters, the games were also held in open spaces within a bustling city.

Most of the time, amphitheaters during the pre-Colosseum era were not built permanently on a specific site; instead, they were temporary structures that could be constructed at any time and dismantled once the games were over. However, when the Romans completed the Theatre of Pompey, temporary amphitheaters became a thing in the past. This was also when Roman amphitheaters were brought to a new height. Commissioned by none other than Gnaeus Pompeius Magnus, better known as Pompey the Great, in 55 BCE, it was Rome's first ever permanent amphitheater made of stone.

Given its massive structure—it was considered the largest in Rome at that time—the Theatre of Pompey was not only used as a gladiatorial arena but also designed for theatrical performances, speeches, and various other cultural events. The amphitheater also grew infamous towards the end of the Roman Republic; this was where the most powerful Roman general and dictator, Julius Caesar, got stabbed twenty-three times by his fellow senators.

Rome was indeed regarded as one of the most colossal empires in the ancient world. The Romans lived, endured, and loved wars. They were known for their military prowess and merciless punishments for those who wronged them. Enemies who refused to bow down to them were put to death, while those had been captured or surrendered were put in chains and sold as slaves.

However, captives, slaves, and prisoners of war deemed strong and possessing mighty figures were put on a different path; these people were sent to gladiatorial schools, where they were trained extensively in combat techniques. Instead of serving their time behind bars (or worse, being slaughtered), these chosen people were expected to put on thrilling performances before crowds of thousands. But, of course, not all gladiators were forced or condemned individuals; many men willingly registered their names as gladiators for personal reasons. Some were looking for fame, while others were searching for a way to escape poverty. At some point, even women joined and fought in the arena.

Contrary to popular belief, a gladiatorial game did not always end with the last person standing. In fact, the outcome of a gladiatorial fight depended on the event organizers, sponsors, or at times, the cheering crowds. Becoming a gladiator warrior did not mean certain death. After all, the gladiator schools owned the fighters, and the cost of hiring a new one to replace the dead was unsurprisingly expensive. Gladiators who survived numerous fights and had served their contracts, on the other hand, were rewarded with freedom. Some gained fortune and fame, while those who wished to stay in the industry were allowed to become trainers.

Perhaps the title of the most renowned figure in the history of gladiatorial combat goes to the Thracian Spartacus. History wrote that Spartacus once served the Eternal City as a soldier but was sold into slavery for his military desertion. He was brought to Capua, where he was forced to train as a gladiator. Not content with his fate, Spartacus and a few other gladiators attempted to escape. This event quickly boiled into something the Romans could never forget. Their attempt was successful, and this act was followed by a series of revolts against the Roman Republic.

Spartacus gathered a small group of followers who had long suffered under the republic. Over time, the number of his followers swelled into an army, allowing them to challenge the might of Rome. With sufficient training and strategies, combined with higher authorities who underestimated their power, Spartacus and his troops successfully defeated several Roman legions. The Roman court soon tasted the impending dangers they would face as long as Spartacus was alive. Only then did they begin to take drastic measures to quell the rebellion.

By 71 BCE, two years following the start of the revolt, Spartacus and his forces were finally defeated at the hands of the Roman general Marcus

Licinius Crassus. Though the fate of Spartacus himself remains uncertain—some suggest he died in battle, while others claim he was captured and executed—the rebellion never had a chance to repeat their successes. Rome never saw another revolt led by discontented gladiators. Though the Roman court gained victory, it was Spartacus who successfully gained immortality; he quickly became a symbol of resistance and freedom, leaving a lasting impact on the Roman psyche.

An illustration depicting Spartacus' supposed death.
https://commons.wikimedia.org/wiki/File:Tod_des_Spartacus_by_Hermann_Vogel.jpg

Nevertheless, the gladiatorial games continued to be immensely popular among the Romans. They eventually became more than a form of entertainment. Especially after the completion of the Colosseum in 80 CE, gladiatorial games were held more often as a display of power and authority of the reigning emperor. The Colosseum also allowed gladiatorial games to reach new heights of extravagance and brutality. Animal hunts became more common, and grand mock naval battles became increasingly popular.

Also known to the ancient Romans as naumachia, mock naval battles were not exclusively held after the completion of the Colosseum. In fact, their origins can be traced to Julius Caesar, who held the first recorded naumachia in 46 BCE. To celebrate his military victories, Caesar had his subjects create a large-scale artificial lake by flooding a basin near the

Tiber River. Here, the mock battle took place, featuring fully equipped ships and thousands of combatants reenacting one of Caesar's naval battles on a grand scale. Caesar was not the only one fond of expensive performances. The first Roman emperor, Augustus, also held his very own naumachia in 2 BCE to celebrate the opening of the Temple of Mars Ultor.

The grandest naumachia ever held, however, was the one hosted by Emperor Claudius in 52 BCE as part of an opening ceremony of a canal later used to dry the Fucine Lake. According to the ancient historian Suetonius, Claudius' naumachia had nearly a hundred ships—triremes and quadriremes—prepared for the mock battle, with over 19,000 slaves dressed in armor, ready (though not willingly) to fight each other.

Naumachiae continued to entertain the Romans after the completion of the Colosseum. With its innovative engineering, the colossal amphitheater could hold elaborate water-based performances. Although the exact methods used to flood and drain the Colosseum's vast arena remain a mystery, many historians and archaeologists have proposed their own theories. One suggestion is that the water was diverted from nearby giant aqueducts into the arena; others proposed that the arena's elaborate drainage system was utilized to flood the space—its sluiced gates were used to flood and drain the arena. Regardless of the technique, the Colosseum was filled with water measuring about five feet deep.

A painting depicting the Roman naumachia.
https://commons.wikimedia.org/wiki/File:La_naumaquia-Ulpiano_Checa.JPG

Since the depth was limited, the Romans had to build miniature boats with flat bottoms, each measuring seven to fifteen meters long. Designed meticulously to resemble the actual warships used in battles, the boats were manned by gladiators in armor who would engage in full-strength combat as if they were indeed fighting for their empire in an actual battle.

It is unknown how many naumachiae were ever held in the Colosseum, as few detailed written records survived the test of time. Emperor Titus was said to have hosted one during the grand opening of the Colosseum. Given Titus' penchant for extravagant displays, it is safe to assume that his naumachia was spectacular, captivating tens of thousands with its scale and spectacle.

Naumachiae never failed to attract huge crowds. However, this form of Roman entertainment was unfortunately rare due to its exorbitant cost. It eventually declined in popularity as time passed. Sources suggested that the last naumachia held in the Colosseum took place in 89 CE and was sponsored by Emperor Domitian. To save money, naumachiae were then commonly staged in lakes as they were before. Since it was less expensive to host them in lakes, naumachiae were probably held there more frequently, though they lacked grandeur. Because of this, the Romans gradually lost interest, favoring other forms of entertainment such as the bloody gladiatorial games, chariot racing, and theatrical performances typically held on land.

Chapter 5 - Petra: A Wonder with Mysterious Beginnings

History has always been entangled with mystery. Archaeologists and historians may find new artifacts that could lead them to a new discovery or perhaps unlock a better understanding of a certain period and civilizations of the past. However, most of these discoveries grant us more questions than answers. The ancient city of Petra is one of the best examples of a wonder that still plagues historians with mysteries.

Many centuries ago, trade was considered a crucial part of the economies and development of ancient civilizations. A small kingdom could bloom into a full-fledged empire through successful trading. Those who held power and controlled the many trade routes and ports had the utmost ability to control the entire world. Spices, exotic animals, gems, and silk were commonly traded throughout this period, but incense quickly grew popular and soon became an important commodity in the ancient world. Not only limited to religious ceremonies, incense was also used in various other ways. Some, especially the ancient Egyptians, used it while embalming the dead and mummifying them. Believed to have healing properties, incense was also valued as a form of medication. Others used it to enhance the taste of wine. As the demand for incense boomed, kingdoms that controlled the incense trade were guaranteed centuries of pouring wealth.

The ancient kingdom of Saba (or Sheba, according to biblical and Quranic references), for one, quickly became the wealthiest kingdom in southern Arabia due to its monopoly on the incense trade. Two of the most valuable types of incense at the time were frankincense and myrrh, which were cultivated from the trees that typically grew in the desert regions of Oman and Yemen. From these regions, the incense was transported by camel caravans via the incense route, which stretched over two thousand kilometers, linking southern Arabia far into the Mediterranean world. Once the cargo arrived at Gaza, a busy port city at the end of the Mediterranean coast, the precious incense would be prepared for shipment via sea to enter the markets of Greece, Rome, Egypt, and beyond.

Though the rewards were exceptionally high, the journey through the incense route was beyond challenging. Not only did the caravans face attacks from bandits lurking in the shadows of night, but traders must also brave the perilous desert with the threats imposed by mother nature herself. Sandstorms were common, and many perished due to limited resources, especially water. However, one tribe was cunning enough to devise a solution to the obstacles that often slow the movements of their caravans. They were known as the Nabateans.

The origin of the Nabateans is rather obscure. They were thought to be literate, but few historical records produced by the tribe still survive. The Nabateans began appearing on written records sometime in the fourth century BCE, though it is plausible they existed long before that. Nevertheless, historians claim that before establishing their kingdom, the Nabateans were Arabian nomads who came all the way from the Negev Desert. Despite the Nabateans' obscure background, we can be sure that, given their constant move around the region, they familiarized themselves with the natural topography and geography of the incense route.

Just as traversing through the incense route was not an easy feat, a one-way journey to reach the port of Gaza took a minimum of sixty-five days, with merchants stopping at a different city each night. Within these cities, merchants were given a chance to rest without worrying about bandits stealing their cargo; they could conduct business and barter their goods in exchange for water. Water was indeed a crucial supply to the merchants, as it was used to sustain them on their dangerous journey until they reached the next city, where the same process would be repeated. Although these overnight stops inevitably delayed their movement toward their final destination in Gaza, it was absolutely necessary to do so.

The trading business, at that time, was undoubtedly competitive, and the Nabateans were well aware of it. The only way to emerge on top was to defeat time itself. The Nabateans planned to limit their overnight stops, thus cutting their travel time to reach the port. To ensure they always had enough water to sustain their journey, the Nabateans dug cisterns along the route and filled them with precious rainwater. These cisterns were then carefully concealed to avoid other Arabian tribes accessing them. Subtle signs that only the Nabateans would recognize were left along the way to point to the cisterns. With these controlled water supplies, the Nabateans could navigate back and forth along the incense route with ease and in an impressively shorter amount of time.

Through their clever innovation, the Nabateans had successfully established themselves as the preeminent traders of the Arabian Peninsula. Once known as an enigmatic nomadic tribe with an unknown background, the Nabateans amassed so much wealth from their trading activities that they were able to assert their dominance and gained control over several integral cities along the incense route. Haluza, Mamshit, Avdat, and Shivta were some of the cities under the Nabateans that were greatly improved to accommodate the traveling merchants. Forts were then constructed to ensure protection for traders who stopped by. Safety, however, was not without a price; traders who desired the luxury of a peaceful night's sleep had to pay a nominal tax.

After being rewarded with such great fortune and crowned as the masters of trade, the Nabateans left their past. From a tribe of wandering merchants, they transformed into a prosperous kingdom that laid the foundation of Petra, their first capital city in southern Jordan, which has earned a place in modern times as one of the seven wonders of the new world. Historians and archaeologists alike cannot yet determine when the construction of Petra took place, but surviving records claim that the city had already achieved fame sometime in the fourth century BCE.

When the Nabateans first planned to establish Petra, finding a strategic location was at the top of the list. They valued their fortune in the trade economy, so it was only wise for them to choose a site along the Incense Trade Route where numerous caravans would pass through day and night. However, many may have underestimated the city. Though the site was strategic, the city was built on a barren desert with nothing but rocky cliffs and a scorching sun burning in the skies. But the Nabateans were highly innovative and gifted builders. They engineered a system to harness the rainwater that came in winter to sustain their entire city: a network of cisterns was carefully constructed to capture the trapped rainwater and supply it to the many sites of the city, including its grandest temples, houses, theatres, fountains, and other public buildings. Those rocky cliffs, on the other hand, proved useful. They acted as natural fortifications against enemies and bandits who dreamed of benefiting from stealing precious cargo brought in by the merchants.

The Egyptians built pyramids using a combination of limestones and mud bricks, while the Romans were famous for their marble structures and monuments. Although the Nabateans were also exposed to these architectural elements (largely due to the influences brought in by the traveling merchants), they chose to discard the idea of designing their city with traditional building materials in favor of a more audacious approach none had ever attempted before. Instead of quarrying limestones and transporting stone slabs from one town to another, the Nabateans used their natural surroundings. Using the resolute sandstone rocks and cliffs as their canvas, the Nabateans carved their city from scratch. Not merely builders but also exceptional artists, the Nabateans successfully chiseled away at the rocks and sculptured the rough cliffs into some of the most stunning structures unlike any other. These hand-carved buildings were also sturdy enough to withstand earthquakes.

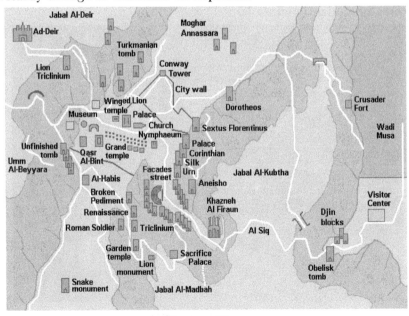

The map of Petra.
https://commons.wikimedia.org/wiki/File:Karta_Petra.PNG

Though built on an empty and dry desert, the city once appeared to be not so much rose red but bright green thanks to the Nabateans' sophisticated network of cisterns, aqueducts, and pipelines that efficiently carried water to irrigate the city's lush gardens, groves, orchards, fountains, and swimming pools. Combining this with its strategic location along the trade route, Petra soon became a bustling trade hub that welcomed merchants and travelers from all over the globe. At its peak, Petra housed over 30,000 citizens of various origins, some of whom were immigrants all the way from Rome, Egypt, Greece, Syria, and Judea.

Once through the narrow gorge called Siq, the main entrance of the ancient city, one could feast one's eyes on the unbelievable sight of the Al-Khazneh, recognized by many historians and scholars from both ancient and modern times as one of the most intricate structures in the desert city. Carved directly into the solid face of the sandstone cliff with exceptional precision and attention to detail, the Al-Khazneh (Arabic for "the Treasury") successfully combined the intricate architectural designs of the indigenous Nabateans with a unique blend of Hellenistic and Egyptian styles. It rose at least forty-three meters above ground and was adorned with elaborate friezes, ornate columns, and decorative motifs, each hand-carved to perfection by the ancient Nabateans using only chisels, hammers, and other hand tools.

The narrow passage, Siq, that leads to Petra.

The purpose of Al-Khazneh, however, remains a subject of debate among archaeologists and historians. Some believe it once served as a ceremonial tomb or mausoleum for important Nabatean figures, most possibly a respected king or queen. The funerary urn crowning the structure further supports this claim. Legend has it that this structure was also used to store precious treasures once belonging to an unknown Egyptian pharaoh. These are nothing more than legends passed down from generation to generation; no treasure has ever been found hidden within the structure. We can never be sure whether there was no treasure or it was already seized by those before us.

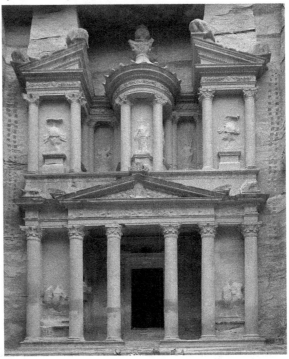

The Treasury.

At Petra, one can also find Ad-Deir ("the Monastery"), another of the several Nabatean wonders. Compared to Al-Khazneh, Ad-Deir was constructed to appear slightly bigger; it rose forty-five meters high and had a width of nearly fifty meters. Based on the carvings of crosses on the walls within the sandstone structure, it is suggestive that Ad-Deir was converted into a church during the era of the Byzantines.

The Ad-Deir.

Just as in the glorious times when Petra was flourishing, as modern-day visitors wind up the ancient streets, they encounter another impressive series of tombs hewn into the rough surface of the rocky massif, Jabal al-Khubtha. These royal tombs—namely, the Urn Tomb, the Silk Tomb, and the Corinthian Tomb—exhibit elaborate facades that precisely reflect the unimaginable wealth of the Nabatean elites buried there.

The Royal Tombs of Petra.

Along the path and south of the Colonnaded Street of Petra was the Great Temple, another of the many architectural marvels hand-carved by the patient Nabateans. Presumably constructed in the early first century CE, the complex served as either a religious site or an administrative center. As with the rest of the structures uncovered in Petra, debate on the exact purpose of the Great Temple has been ongoing. The temple's grandeur and monumental size, however, show significant signs that it was indeed built as a dedication to the Nabatean deities. This site could also be where important ceremonies and gatherings were held. Though what remains of the Great Temple are only colossal columns, remnants of the expansive staircase, and several chambers, the site never fails to leave visitors completely awe-struck.

Ruins of the Great Temple.

Bernard Gagnon, CC BY-SA 3.0 <https://creativecommons.org/licenses/by-sa/3.0>, via Wikimedia Commons: https://commons.wikimedia.org/wiki/File:Great_Temple_of_Petra_02.jpg

Not limited to only the Al-Khazneh, Ad-Deir, the Royal Tombs, and the Great Temple, the rest of the structures scattered throughout Petra's sprawling landscape have proven the rich culture of the Nabateans and their architectural genius. Though forgotten by many following the years when the Romans renamed themselves the Byzantines, Petra was not planning to be buried beneath the dust again. Declared a UNESCO World Heritage Site along with six other wonders of the new world, it will be a long time–or never–before Petra can be forgotten again.

Chapter 6 - Petra: The Envy of the Ancient World's Superpowers

The year was 323 BCE, and the people of Ancient Macedonia were mourning. Their king and the mighty conqueror, Alexander the Great, had just passed away after battling a serious illness that had left him in bed day and night. Though he had a wife—who was pregnant with his first child—the conqueror never named a successor to continue his legacy. And so, his vast empire, which spanned from Greece to Egypt, Persia, and a portion of India, was divided among his most powerful comrades: Ptolemy, Seleucus, Cassander, and Antigonus. These generals each gained control over different territories and often waged war with each other. However, Antigonus was widely considered the greatest success of the four.

Antigonus had been swaying his sword on the battlefield and commanding the Macedonian phalanx since the reign of King Philip II, the father of Alexander the Great. Beginning his career as a mere soldier, Antigonus rose through the ranks and eventually became one of Philip's most trusted advisors. It was also during a battle under Philip's rule that Antigonus received a terrible blow across his face. As a result, he lost his right eye; after that, he was known as Antigonus the One-Eyed.

With or without his right eye, Antigonus was never known to back down; he continued leading his troops in many more campaigns, each far more dangerous than the previous. After Philip's death, Antigonus continued to serve under Alexander and was appointed as a general in the army who was absolutely instrumental in securing Alexander's victories in both Persia and Egypt.

As an ambitious and ruthless ruler, Antigonus dreamed of reuniting the great empire once established by Alexander, and he planned to rule it alone. And so, he began expanding his domain, the Antigonid dynasty. With careful planning and execution, he quickly swept across Syria and conquered the Mediterranean coast. Military campaigns were no doubt expensive, and his rapid expansion had, of course, drained his coffers. Thus, he decided to hungrily shift his focus to Petra—a city he deemed extremely wealthy—that could be greatly useful for his empire's conquest.

Sometime in 312 BCE, Antigonus sent one of his trusted generals, Athenaeus, to the dry lands of the Nabateans with a mission to secure their vast resources and riches. Backed up by four thousand light foot soldiers, some of whom had served under Alexander and six hundred horsemen, Athenaeus marched out of Judea and into the merciless desert en route to plunder as much Nabatean wealth as his animals could carry.

It took them three days before they could set eyes on the Rose City. Noticing how busy Petra could be during the day, Athenaeus ordered his troops to set camp and wait for nightfall. As soon as the dark shadows of night covered the entire rock-cut city, Athenaeus and his army made a move. Under the cover of darkness, they stormed the quiet city. There was little resistance, as most Nabatean men had gone on the road to conduct business. Women and children were caught by surprise by the attack. The silence of the dark night was replaced by screaming and pleas as the troops went into a frenzy; they looted all the riches they could find and obliterated those who dared to stand in their way.

Before word about their sudden attack could reach the traveling Nabatean men, Athenaeus and his men quickly loaded their horses and carts with as much loot as they could plunder. Ancient sources state that they left Petra with countless precious trade goods, including frankincense, myrrh, and nearly fourteen tons of silver. Frightened women and children were also taken and put in shackles with the intention of selling them as slaves.

Content with all the fortune they had amassed from the easy ambush, Athenaeus and his men were confident they had accomplished their mission. And so, they set up another camp about thirty-six kilometers away from Petra, where they spent the night. One little mistake they overlooked, however, was the ones who were left wounded in the city.

A few hours after Athenaeus' departure, the first few Nabatean men arrived in Petra. They were, of course, beyond surprised by the sight of their city. Their homes and holy temples were ransacked, and their families were nowhere to be found. At first, these men had zero idea of the culprit behind this tragedy. That was, until they started tending to the wounded. Fighting the pain inflicted by their wounds, the survivors told the Nabatean men of Athenaeus' attack. This information no doubt stoked the flames of anger and vengeance. In a matter of hours, the Nabatean men had armed themselves and mounted their camels, ready to set out and track down the cowardly invaders. As they rode through nearby settlements and villages, they rallied more and more warriors to their cause, swelling their numbers to eight thousand armed camel riders.

Athenaeus and his men had no idea what was coming for them. They spent the night sleeping with little thought of possible retaliation. As they were sleeping soundly, their prisoners were said to have successfully sneaked out of the camp undetected. The eight thousand camel riders arrived at the camp by nightfall. Perhaps learning from the Antigonids, they used the cover of darkness and laid a surprise attack. Using javelins, the Nabateans slaughtered their enemies. Those who were deep asleep died without having the chance to defend themselves, while those who had their swords were quickly dealt with. Out of all, only fifty horsemen managed to escape the attack—though they, too, were terribly injured. With this victory, the Nabateans successfully reclaimed what was theirs; all of the stolen wealth was brought back to the city along with the captured prisoners, women, and children.

Despite their prowess in battle, the Nabateans were, in fact, peaceful people and had no desire for further bloodshed. Seeking to avoid any unnecessary conflict, they wrote a letter in Aramaic (the region's lingua franca) and sent it to Antigonus, explaining the circumstances that had led to the slaughter of Athenaeus and his men. To their surprise, Antigonus showed signs of understanding and excused them for the killings. Though he was trying to project his image as a calm ruler during this exchange, Antigonus had no intention of leaving the Nabateans alone. He knew they were a proud people who valued their independence above all, so the Antigonid king sought to placate them with promises of peace and security. In his reply, he assured the Nabateans that there would be no war following the massacre.

Although partly relieved by Antigonus' response, the Nabateans could not afford to be caught off-guard again. Despite the king's assurances, they remained skeptical and maintained their guard, stationing sentries along the borders and atop the cliffs to watch for any sign of foreign aggression.

Their suspicions proved to be well-founded. Antigonus, determined to succeed where Athenaeus had failed, dispatched his son Demetrius with an army of another four thousand skilled soldiers to Petra. However, the Nabatean watchmen were quick to spot the Antigonid army from afar and immediately set fire to warning beacons placed on hilltops throughout the region. They gathered their families and valuables and retreated to a stony fortress that historians believe was carved into Petra's highest point, the mountain Umm Al-Biyara.

Learning of their retreat, Demetrius and his soldiers laid an assault on the fortress, but its natural defenses made the attack impossible. The narrow crevices leading up to the fortress would be deadly for his soldiers to navigate, and besieging it was not an option as the Nabateans had their own secret supplies of water. Demetrius was, indeed, on the brink of defeat, but he refused to return empty-handed.

Unbeknownst to the Antigonids, the Nabateans were not only cunning fighters but also gifted in the art of negotiations. As Demetrius led his army in another attempt to breach the impregnable fortress, a shrewd Nabatean stepped forward to speak. He first questioned Antigonus' motive for invading them, arguing that their city was built far into the desert and posed no threat to anyone. He stated that his people were not planning to harm others, as they wished only to carry on with their lives in peace. The man then laid out his negotiation terms: the Nabateans would gift the Antigonids with generous riches if they retreated to where they belonged and maintained a friendly relationship with the Nabateans.

The Antigonids, whose supplies began to deplete, had no choice but to agree to the offer. Demetrius accepted the handsome gifts and led his troops back to their homeland, though he was not pleased with the outcome. Upon receiving the reports of the failed invasion, Antigonus was said by the historian Diodorus to have expressed his anger towards his son. Despite returning from Arabia much richer, the Antigonids were far from victory. Antigonus claimed that his son had allowed the barbaric Nabateans to grow even bolder. Nevertheless, the Antigonids unintentionally stayed true to their promise after all; eventually, Antigonus was forced to abandon his plans on Petra as he needed to settle internal matters.

The Nabateans and their Rose City were spared from war and bloodshed. But, as their wealth grew each year, they attracted another colossal power of the ancient world: this time, it was the Roman Empire, which had just expanded its realm to Egypt.

One of the reasons behind their plan to conquer the Nabateans was the rich incense fields of Arabia. The Romans were religious people and one of the largest consumers of incense. Frankincense was burned in their many temples, and the Romans also constantly used myrrh as part of their religious rituals. As the empire experienced rapid expansion and its population grew, it was estimated that over a million kilograms of frankincense were imported from Arabia. In the eyes of the reigning emperor, Augustus Caesar, the cost of the import was draining his coffers, especially when the Nabateans had imposed a 25 percent tax on the goods. And so, Augustus sought ways to minimize his vast empire's spending; instead of negotiating, he planned to get his hands on the incense trade route.

However, one problem loomed over his head—the Romans were not perfectly familiar with the territories of Southern Arabia. Therefore, Augustus sent Aelius Gallus, his trusted prefect in charge of Roman Egypt, to explore the lay of the land and establish new trade routes that would connect them to the locals. Equipped with only a small force, Aelius Gallus led the expedition until it was met with a warm welcome by the Nabateans.

Surprisingly, the Nabateans maintained friendly communication with the Romans—they even provided one of their own as a guide for the Romans' exploration. According to the Greek geographer and historian Strabo, instead of having their guards up, the Romans were pleased with the supposed cooperation of the Nabateans and let themselves be guided by one of the locals sent by the Nabatean king. Little did they know, their guide was not merely a humble man who knew his map. Introducing himself as Syllaeus, the man held a high political position in the court of the Nabatean government. Before meeting with the Romans, who were more than eager to continue their expedition, Syllaeus had been strictly tasked by his king to do nothing but two things: he was to put on a mask and appear cooperative to the Romans while at the same time ensuring the expedition went south.

Syllaeus was undoubtedly put in a dangerous position. One wrong step, and he would face the wrath of the colossal empire. If he failed to mislead the Romans, Syllaeus might have his head served on a silver platter by the Nabatean king. Nevertheless, Syllaeus accomplished his tasks. He used the trust the Romans had in him and guided them through a long, perilous journey along the coast of southern Arabia. There were easier routes to Petra usually used by Arab traders, but Syllaeus managed to conceal this information.

Many of Gallus' men succumbed to their deaths during the six-month journey. Their lives were either taken by serious diseases, heat stroke, fatigue, or poisonous herbs and tainted water consumed along the way. The Romans were most likely traveling in circles, though every once in a while, Syllaeus would lead them on the right course so that he would not raise their suspicions. Only when his forces were severely depleted did Gallus admit defeat and announce that he would return to the empire.

Without delaying a single minute, Aelius Gallus led what remained of his troops back home, retracing the steps they had taken using the guidance of Syllaeus. At some point during his retreat, Gallus finally realized he had been tricked—informed by his captives. He could have spent only two days to reach Petra, but Syllaeus had successfully extended the journey. It is uncertain when Syllaeus made his quiet escape—it is safe to assume Syllaeus was not present when the Romans realized his tricks—but the Romans had returned to Alexandria with nothing but a pair of empty hands.

The Nabateans and Petra were spared yet again following Syllaeus' tricks. Like centuries before, Petra enjoyed its independence as the Romans had their hands full with a series of civil wars. About a century later, they would return; by 106 CE, the Romans successfully paid their vengeance. Petra and its surrounding territories were invaded and annexed into the empire, which changed the province's name to Arabia Petraea. From this moment on, the Romans would rule Petra for 250 years.

The Roman annexation was the beginning of an end for Petra and the Nabateans. As Christianity began to spread widely across the Roman Empire, the use of incense deteriorated; thus, Petra no longer enjoyed being the most popular trade hub. The once glorious city was also affected by the Galilee earthquake in 363 CE, resulting in the destruction of nearly half of its magnificent structures.

Two years after the unforgettable natural disaster, Petra was forced to endure a siege by the Byzantines under Emperor Justinian I. The Nabateans' defeat put them in the hands of the Byzantines, who would rule over them for three hundred years. By the eighth century CE, Petra almost completely fell into disuse. Since its location was no longer considered strategically important, Petra was abandoned, with its remaining structures inhabited by only nomadic shepherds. As the nomads moved on, Petra was reclaimed by the dust of the desert—left forgotten and hidden from the eyes of the Europeans.

That was, until 1812 when the explorer John Lewis Burckhardt rediscovered the city. Since then, the stone city has been exclusively put onto the world stage of archeology. Countless scholars, historians, and archaeologists visited the site, studying and admiring the wondrous city of the Nabateans. Though no longer carrying the title of the wealthiest city, Petra's historical and cultural significance grew, forever solidifying its position as one of the world's most remarkable ancient cities. Its rose-colored sandstone structures, hidden passages and crevices, and awe-inspiring landscapes continue to captivate visitors, transporting them back to an era when Petra flourished as a thriving center of trade and culture.

Chapter 7 - The Arrival of the Portuguese along the Shores of Brazil

By the end of the 15th century CE, the world had just begun to witness the start of a transformative era. Known in historical terms as the Age of Discovery, this was a time when European nations actively embarked on multiple series of voyages and expeditions in search of new trade routes and wealth. Among the many explorers frequently scouring through the ocean were the Portuguese, whose exceptional maritime prowess had turned them into one of the most formidable powers in European history.

In the early 15th century CE, Portuguese explorers were put under the leadership of Prince Henry the Navigator; their aim was to explore the undiscovered coast of Africa. And so, once disembarked from the harbor and the heavy anchor hoisted, the Portuguese, with eyes filled with determination, set sail across the sea, advancing farther south than any previous expeditions held by other European superpowers. After enduring all sorts of challenges in the ocean, including storms, diseases, and perhaps a few equipment failures, the Portuguese successfully mapped a good portion of western Africa. In 1488, they finally witnessed a greater achievement: Bartolomeu Dias had successfully become the first European to sail around the southern tip of Africa, known as the Cape of Good Hope. His success brought European maritime expeditions to a greater height as, a decade later, another Portuguese explorer named

Vasco da Gama found a passage to reach India. This allowed the Europeans to establish a direct sea connection with the vast markets of the East.

Apart from the Portuguese Empire, Spain never failed to showcase its exploration skills in the Age of Discovery. Once done with the Reconquista (the Reconquest of Spain), campaigns that involved countless wars spanning over seven centuries, the Spanish could finally shift their attention to expanding their realm. They were indeed hungry for more lands, resources, and attractive wealth, typically hidden in the Far East.

Among the many explorers and seafarers aboard the ships carrying the flags of European countries, one particular figure hailing from Italy dreamed of being the first to set foot on the shores of Asia. His name was Christopher Columbus. After years of calculations, studies, and observation of the endless ocean, Columbus arrived at a conclusion that not everyone would nod to: he claimed there was an easy passage to Asia. By sailing west across the Atlantic instead of going around Africa, he could reach Asia with minimal time and difficulties.

Confident in his calculations, Columbus first proposed the idea to the Portuguese, proposing they fund his expedition. They immediately refused to lend him their support. Not planning to give up, the Italian explorer turned to the Spanish monarchs—Ferdinand and Isabella—who agreed to a sponsorship.

And so, Columbus embarked on a mission to prove his claim and discover new parts of the globe. He sailed across the Atlantic in 1492 until he finally docked at a Caribbean island, believing he had just discovered a western trade route to India and China. Upon nearing land, he mistakenly claimed that he had arrived on the eastern shores of Asia.

Columbus returned to Spain to inform his sponsors of the New World he had set his eyes on. Christopher Columbus was widely regarded as the first European to set foot on the New World. However, few knew that the title had already been given to Leif Erikson, a Norse explorer whose adventure took place nearly half a millennium before Columbus' birth. Regardless, the news brought back by Columbus immediately sparked a colossal wave of excitement among the European powers as they began planning ways to capitalize and benefit from the new-found lands.

Following Columbus' voyage, representatives from Spain and Portugal gathered to discuss which indigenous lands of the new world were located in whose territory. To resolve the matter, the two European nations signed the Treaty of Tordesillas, which divided the newly discovered lands between the two powers. Through the treaty, they established an imaginary line called the Line of Demarcation, which divided the lands of the Americas into separate spheres of influence. While Spain was granted rights to explore lands west of the line, Portugal was given those to the east.

As such, King Manuel I of Portugal, who was driven by ambitions, wealth, and power, set his eyes on colonizing as many lands as possible on the east of the imaginary line. One of the lands that would soon be added to the list was none other than Brazil.

The following years were filled by a race of expeditions sent out by these two rival powers. In 1500 CE, a Portuguese expedition under the leadership of Pedro Alvares Cabral had just left Lisbon with an initial aim to reach the East Indies. Several historical accounts suggest that Cabral intended to retrace the steps taken by Vasco da Gama during his unforgettable voyage around the Cape of Good Hope. However, unprecedented storms and navigational errors soon foiled his plans. Cabral and his team of explorers veered off-course and eventually made landfall at a location known to us today as Porto Seguro in northern Brazil. While these sources clearly suggest that Cabral had no prior knowledge of Brazil's existence, many claimed his arrival was intentional.

Regardless of the claims, Cabral was said to have not jumped onto the shores of Porto Seguro right away. Upon noticing inhabitants going about their lives on the shores from a distance, Cabral gathered the captains of his three ships for a discussion. He then ordered the captain, Nicolau Coelho, who had earned a name in the maritime industry for his participation in Vasco da Gama's expedition to India, to travel ashore and make contact with the locals—perhaps to see whether the locals were hostile to foreign faces. Without question, Coelho did what he was asked, and, fortunately, the locals maintained friendly expressions. They exchanged gifts, and it was only after Coelho's return to his ship that Cabral ordered his fleet to dock at Porto Seguro.

In return for the Portuguese's friendly introduction, the locals were pleased to show them around, providing information about their tribes. Most were hunter-gatherers to whom the Europeans had assigned the collective label "Indians." Men in these groups sustained their diet by hunting big game animals, fishing, and foraging, while women were often engaged in small-scale agriculture. There were multiple tribes inhabiting the land—some of whom practiced cannibalism—and the one who made contact with Cabral is believed to have belonged to the Tupiniquim tribe.

Cabral did not prolong his stay in Brazil; the Portuguese remained not more than ten days before setting on another journey to obtain the lucrative possessions of Africa and India. At the moment, the Portuguese paid little attention to Brazil. They would only return to the coasts to get brazilwood, often used by the Europeans to produce valuable red dyes for luxury textiles. The Portuguese were actively engaged in trade with the Brazilian tribes, as they had to rely on them to extract the brazilwood from the dense jungle. In return, the tribes obtained mirrors, scissors, knives, and axes from the Europeans.

It was only when the precious wood caught the attention of the French that the Portuguese Crown began to take action. By that time, the presence of the French had grown tremendously. And so, in 1530, a Portuguese expedition was dispatched to Brazil to patrol the coast. Spearheaded by Martim Afonso de Sousa, the Portuguese expelled the French and eventually established their first colonial villages along the coast.

Certain scholars claim that Brazil was thought of more as a lucrative commercial asset than a region to be settled. However, the Portuguese Crown eventually figured that having Brazil serve only as a trading post was not ideal; thus, they began to get deeper into the region's organizational structure. To ensure Brazil was always under their close watch, the Portuguese introduced a system of hereditary captaincies in which the territories were divided and overseen by high-ranking officials well-connected to the Portuguese Crown. The Portuguese nobleman, Duarte Coelho, for instance, was granted Pernambuco, a region that prospered by the cultivation of sugarcane and cotton. On the other hand, São Vicente, the first permanent Portuguese settlement, soon became a hub for indigenous slave trafficking.

In 1549, Brazil was met with the arrival of Tomé de Sousa, who established a central government. Arriving along the shores with him were the Jesuit priests, a Catholic religious order tasked with spreading Christianity in Brazil.

The Jesuits worked to accomplish their mission almost as soon as they arrived in Brazil. They established "reductions," mission towns, across the many regions of Brazil. Converting the indigenous people of Brazil was undoubtedly easier said than done. And so, the Jesuits tried approaching them not only to introduce their religious teachings but also to improve their living conditions and their entire well-being. The Jesuits opened the reductions to all locals, providing medical assistance to those in need while introducing them to new agricultural techniques to enhance the production of their crops. The Jesuits believed that education was essential for a person's spiritual and intellectual development. Thus, apart from churches, they built a few schools, which were typically used by the missionaries to provide education to the children of both the indigenous tribes and Portuguese settlers.

However, the locals were not the only ones learning; the Jesuits also spent their days and nights perfecting their skills in the native languages spoken by the indigenous people. With fluency in their mother tongue, the Jesuits could translate religious texts for the locals to better understand their teachings.

The Jesuits received the utmost support from the Portuguese Crown; by spreading Christianity all over the territory, the Portuguese thought it would be easier to consolidate their power. Thus, the missionaries were given more than enough financial and logistical assistance and legal protection for their roles. New policies were also introduced to ensure not a single local was excluded from Catholic teachings. This policy encouraged the indigenous people to set up their dwellings close to the missions.

Of course, converting the people of the Brazilian territory was not a walk in the park; there were multiple challenges and conflicts the Jesuits were forced to deal with. Not all locals were content with the arrival of a religion completely new to them. Many refused to convert, preferring to cling to their spiritual beliefs and centuries-long cultural practices. Mere arguments and minor clashes between indigenous traditions and Catholic teaching sometimes became serious tensions and conflicts. The diseases brought in by the foreigners, combined with forced labor imposed by the Portuguese colonial enterprises, further led the locals to turn away from Catholicism.

Despite the issues and obstacles, the Jesuits eventually witnessed a significant change in Brazilian society. More indigenous populations gradually chose to embrace aspects of Catholicism, merging some of their traditional beliefs with Christian rituals and practices. The Jesuit missions prospered and turned into important centers of religious and cultural exchange.

Over the centuries, Christianity continued to bloom all over Brazil, eventually shaping the religious, cultural, and architectural landscape of the region. Four centuries following the first arrival of the Portuguese Jesuits, Brazil became the home to one of the most iconic symbols in Christianity. The statue of Christ the Redeemer would soon rest atop the highest peak of Rio de Janeiro, overseeing the land and ocean surrounding it.

Chapter 8 - Christ the Redeemer: Brazil's Symbol of Faith

During the 19th century, particularly in the 1850s, a local priest was the first to propose the idea of building a colossal Christian monument in Rio, the capital of Brazil at the time. His proposal was presented out of a desire to honor the royal family, specifically Princess Isabel, the daughter of Emperor Pedro II and Empress Teresa Cristina. Recognizing the importance of the statue—to serve as a tribute to the monarchy and to emphasize the presence of Christianity in Brazil—the priest also voiced the idea of erecting the statue on Mount Corcovado, which geographically provides a strong presence for the statue and ensures its visibility from various locations throughout Rio de Janeiro.

Unfortunately, the idea to build the Christian monument faced various obstacles that eventually led to its cancellation. Some of the problems were the lack of funding and the political changes most likely brought by the Proclamation of the Republic in 1889—the creation of a republican government after ending the Brazilian monarchy.

A view of Mount Corcovado before the construction of Christ the Redeemer.
https://commons.wikimedia.org/wiki/File:Corcovadoporferrez.jpg

However, following the end of World War I, the idea of building such a monumental statue was picked up again. This time, it was proposed by the Roman Catholic archdiocese in Rio. The leaders were concerned about the state of Brazilians, who were thought to have gradually lost their religious faith. And so, in 1923, t to realize the project's construction, the Brazilians held a fundraising campaign. Referred to as "Monument Week," the campaign was well-received by the people and successfully garnered half of what was required to lay the project's foundation. However, building such a grand structure was easier said than done; it was not until a few years later that the construction work could finally begin.

Although the exact number of people who worked on the construction was not historically documented in writing, it is safe to assume that the work required hundreds of hands. Nevertheless, it is worth noting that three key figures worked tirelessly year after year to turn the Catholics' vision into reality. These men were Heitor da Silva Costa, Gheorghe Leonida, and Paul Landowski.

Like any monument ever built, the process of designing the statue was extensive; the first few sketches of Christ of Redeemer went through several revisions before it reached its final form. Heitor was the one who had been working tirelessly to create the best design for the statue. At first, he envisioned the monument to appear extravagant in its pose; his first sketch was of Jesus clasping an enormous cross against his body and his other hand holding a globe. He also planned to have the statue face in the direction of the rising sun.

Unfortunately, for unspecified reasons, the design was scrapped. Some suggest the design was too complex for construction on top of a mountain; others put the blame on an insufficient budget. Nevertheless, Heitor eventually came up with another idea that earned the green light.

Primarily influenced by the Art Deco style first introduced in France in the early 1920s, Heitor drew inspiration from the radio antennas that stop atop Mount Corcovado. He was further advised by the artist Carlos Oswald to have the statue's body act as a cross. And so, the design of Christ the Redeemer was finalized. The giant statue would have both of its arms extended as if it was embracing and welcoming people into Rio de Janeiro.

Christ the Redeemer alongside a set of antennas that inspired Heitor da Silva Costa.
Diego Torres Silvestre from Sao Paulo, Brazil, CC BY 2.0
<https://creativecommons.org/licenses/by/2.0>, via Wikimedia Commons:
https://commons.wikimedia.org/wiki/File:(2006)_Christ_the_Redeemer_(6955601775).jpg

Heitor might have played a crucial role in designing the overall look of the statue; however, the face of the sculpture was handled by Gheorghe Leonida, a talented and skilled artist who hailed from Romania. Leonida's task was to not only produce a sculpture with extreme precision but also capture the sense of warmth and spirituality of Christ in his work.

To breathe life into the Deco style of the statue, Heitor worked hand-in-hand with Paul Landowski, a French-Polish sculptor, who was put in charge of ensuring the overall aesthetic of the statue. Perhaps in his workshop in Paris, Landowski sculpted the statue's head and hands in their real measurement; sources claim the sculptor spent at least a few years perfecting a four-meter plaster model of the statue in his studio. Once completed, these clay sculptures were sent to Rio by boat. Only then would the craftsmen in Brazil work to reproduce the concrete models of the clay sculpture carved by Landowski—this process is said to have taken an extensive number of hours.

The statue's construction was still far from completion when Heitor was met with another challenge: the Brazilian engineer had to finalize the external finish of the statue. He was well aware that using concrete alone would not give the grand statue the astonishing finishing effect he had long envisioned. And so, he embarked on yet another quest to solve the problem.

Heitor soon got inspiration during his visit to a recently opened arcade in Champs-Elysees. Here, he was left fascinated by a Parisian fountain that had its walls lined with mosaics made of tiny, triangular tiles. With this fresh idea, Heitor experimented with various materials to determine the best choice for his grand statue. He eventually settled on soapstone, which was already commonly used in the many churches of Brazil. Soapstone was also popularly known for its resistance to fading, sun, and rain and withstand temperature fluctuations.

Later, the society women of the churches gathered to lend their hands to completing the meticulous structure. For hours, they worked together to stick the triangular pieces of soapstone to sheets of mesh, which would later be used to cover every part of the body of Christ—except the head and hands. Some said that the women would even write the names of their loved ones on the back of the triangular pieces before attaching the tile to the mesh sheets. This, they believed, would forever seal their love.

Without a doubt, constructing a gigantic monument on top of a mountain rising to a great height was not simple. In fact, many had wondered about the process of placing such a statue on the summit. Interestingly, the statue was not placed on the mountain all at once; instead, pieces of it were assembled on the mountaintop. Once they checked off all the materials needed for the construction—including the mesh sheets full of the triangular soapstone tiles—they transported these items to the construction site perched on the mountain. Special care was taken to ensure the safe transport of these delicate materials. A single crack in the concrete sculpture would definitely delay the construction work.

These materials were transported using a cogwheel train—the same one reserved for tourists who wish to explore the summit without climbing the steep paths. Water, on the other hand, was hauled from a fountain almost three hundred meters from the construction site. By scaling the scaffoldings, skilled workers would carefully lift and position the heavy pieces of the statues, which were installed with precise alignment and stability. Once the workers were done with the concrete structure, another team of craftsmen would use their precision skills to cover the entire statue with the triangular soapstone pieces. It is estimated that over six million pieces of tiny soapstone mosaic tiles were used.

The construction of Christ the Redeemer began in the middle of 1926 and took nine long years to complete. Unlike other colossal structures of ancient times, no lives were lost during the entire construction process despite all the significant challenges of working at such a great height.

On the 12th of October, 1931, the statue began receiving its first sets of visitors. A large gathering of tourists and locals, government representatives, and religious leaders gathered on top of Mount Corcovado to witness the inauguration of the grand statue. Towering over thirty meters tall—making it the third tallest statue of Christ in the world— the statue's outstretched arms span over twenty-eight meters. Combined with the panoramic views of Rio de Janeiro, the statue of Christ the Redeemer has become a famous landmark in Brazil, enthralling millions of tourists hailing from each continent.

The panoramic view of Christ the Redeemer atop Mount Corcovado.

Nevertheless, the statue was also not free from the clasp of disaster. Due to its location at the peak of a mountain, the majestic monument had to face the fury of mother nature. Over the years, the statue was forced to endure strong winds, heavy rainfall, and of course, terrifying lightning strikes. In fact, the statue has been struck by lightning several times during its existence. Fortunately, Brazil spared no expense to bring the statue back to its former glory. Despite the formidable natural obstacles, Christ the Redeemer remains on top of the mountain, posing as a symbol of unwavering faith and hopeful aspiration.

Chapter 9 - The Conquest of the Inca: Triumphs and Tragedies

Every man in the world craves power. Whether weak or strong, rich or poor, young or old—all have the ambition of having the world wrapped around their precious fingers. The same could be said for Francisco Pizarro, the Spanish conquistador, or conqueror, whose name rose to fame in 1532 upon his success at obliterating the Inca civilization. Unlike many powerful figures immortalized in history books today, Pizarro was not born with a silver spoon. He was, in fact, born into a rather humble family. Though his father served in the Spanish army as a colonel, his family was not wealthy, and his mother was described as the daughter of a mere farmer. Pizarro never had the chance to attend school, and he was believed to have grown up without knowing how to read or write.

Despite his unfair early years, Pizarro was always intrigued by tales of adventures in the New World. His urge to create a name of his own soon grew so strong that, in 1502, he left his home in Trujillo and embarked on a journey of fame and fortune. He first set sail to the Spanish colony of Hispaniola (modern-day Dominican Republic). Seven years later, Pizarro found himself in a failed expedition to the New World led by Alonso de Ojeda. It was only in 1513 that he began to take a step closer to the fortune he desired: Pizarro successfully rose as a captain under an expedition led by Vasco Nuñez de Balboa and became one of the first Europeans to set eyes on the Pacific Ocean. Panama soon became his home, where he obtained a successful political position and indulged in great wealth. Now a powerful mayor of Panama, it was high time for Pizarro to launch his own expedition and realize his dreams of having his name remembered by generations to come.

Obsessed with rumors of a thriving empire tucked in the obscure lands of South America, Pizarro worked to raise funds for his dream expedition. In 1524, he set sail to the northern coast of South America to confirm the rumors that had kept him awake most nights. However, it went south faster than he could gain information: many of his men were killed, while Pizarro suffered several wounds. A few years later, he launched another expedition against the wishes of the governor of Panama, who had begun losing faith in him. Nevertheless, his effort was fruitful this time. Pizarro and his men discovered the bustling town of Tumbes, which confirmed the rumors all along: a great civilization was blooming. And most importantly, they possessed an unthinkable amount of gold and silver.

To take on the mysterious natives right there and then would undoubtedly be suicide. And so, Pizarro packed his bags and returned to Spain, where he arranged a meeting with the king of Spain, Holy Roman Emperor Charles V. Supported by the newly discovered evidence, Pizarro presented the benefits of controlling Peru to the Spanish crown. Impressed, the king granted royal approval for the ambitious expedition. Pizarro was tasked with forming new colonies on the new lands and spreading Christianity. In return, Pizarro was made governor of all the lands he would be conquering and allowed to keep four-fifths of the wealth he would soon seize.

With the royal permission proudly in his hands, Pizarro returned to Trujillo and checked the first task off his list: enlisting reliable conquistadors to accompany his mission. His four paternal brothers, Juan, Francisco, Gonzalo, and Hernando, were among them. They boarded their ships in January 1540 en route to the Americas.

However, unbeknownst to the Spaniards, the Inca civilization was already battling a series of conflicts.

Several years before the arrival of the Spaniards, the empire was ruled by Huayna Capac, who gained the throne as the Sapa Inka (the monarch of the Inca Empire) in 1493. Although the Inca Empire was already at its height, largely thanks to his predecessor, Huayna Capac soon received daunting news that would mark the beginning of the empire's decline. Every day, the Sapan Inka received chasquis (Inca runners) who carried reports of the deaths of thousands in the north. They were believed to have succumbed to a mysterious disease that none of the Incas were familiar with. It arrived on the Inca lands a few years before Pizarro and his band of men could set their base for their conquest mission; the disease came from North and Central America.

Known to us today as smallpox, the Eurasian disease ravaged the Inca population as if there was no tomorrow. Sometime in 1528, those spared from the plague mourned the death of their Sapan Inka, Huayna Capac, who, along with his heir, was finally defeated by the merciless disease. With the deaths of millions, the sickness had unintentionally sided with Pizarro. Two years before he met with the Spanish king, the Inca had already lost nearly 90 percent of its population.

Left without a ruler, the Inca Empire was thrown into six years of turmoil as civil war erupted between the two remaining sons of Huayna Capac: Atahualpa and Huascar. While Huascar had his hands on most regions of the empire, Atahualpa gained support from his late father's veteran legions. And so, Atahualpa wasted no time leaving his seat in Quito and setting camp in Cajamarca. Bloodshed soon took over the empire as the civil war continued without rest. It finally ended in 1532 when Huascar's army was heavily defeated by Atahualpa's right outside Cuzco (the Incan capital). Huascar himself was captured, thus leaving the throne to Atahualpa.

Word of Huascar's defeat is said to have reached Atahualpa five days following the bloody battle—the chasquis delivered messages only by foot. Upon hearing the victory, Atahualpa again wasted no time planning his coronation. This, however, was not the only news he had received from the chasquis: the local chiefs had spotted 168 foreigners arriving on the shores of their land, with some riding "giant llamas." Atahualpa was also informed that these peculiar men were already en route to Cajamarca. Curious about the foreigners and their giant llamas—the Incas were not familiar with horses at the time—Atahualpa decided to meet them.

It is said that Pizarro and Atahualpa met twice. The first meeting was in mid-November 1532, and it was rather friendly. After all, the Sapan Inka was in a convivial mood following his victory in the civil war. Drinks were poured, speeches were exchanged, and the Incas got up close to the horses, a type of creature new to their realm. However, Pizarro never intended to maintain his friendly manner. The very next day, the Spaniards planned to launch a surprise attack against the Incas under the disguise of a celebration. Pizarro had arrived in Peru a year before the end of the civil war and had been waiting for a golden opportunity to begin his conquest. Knowing Atahualpa had just ascended to the throne, the Spaniard invited the Sapan Inka to a feast to honor his victory. The supposed celebration was held at the main plaza of Cajamarca.

At that time, Atahualpa controlled over 80,000 men. Sensing no hostility, the Sapan Inka agreed to attend the feast. He brought 5,000 men, who were only armed with a single axe. Unbeknownst to them, Pizarro had carefully planned an ambush—the conquistador had hidden his heavily-armed men around the plaza. When Atahualpa arrived, he was greeted by the Dominican friar, Vicente de Valverde, who was also accompanied by a native translator.

The friar urged Atahualpa to accept Charles V as sovereign and to embrace Christianity. Sources claim that the friar went to the extent of threatening the Sapan Inka. The friar insisted that destruction was inevitable should the Sapan Inka refuse to convert to Christianity. Deaths following his stubbornness would also be entirely his fault. These words were a part of the Requerimiento, a document that proclaimed Spain's divine rights to conquests in the name of God. Perhaps feeling deceived, Atahualpa did the very thing Pizarro had hoped for: he angrily refused to fulfill the Spaniards' demands. And so, Pizarro signaled his men to emerge from their hiding and open fire, prompting the start of the famed Massacre of Cajamarca.

A depiction of the Massacre of Cajamarca.
https://commons.wikimedia.org/wiki/File:Inca-Spanish_confrontation.JPG

Trapped in the middle of the plaza with only narrow exits and armed with minimal weapons, the Inca warriors were easy prey to the Spaniards. Pizarro's small forces of 168 men shouted their battle cry "Santiago!" and, with their advanced weaponry, slaughtered the panicking Incas in just over an hour. All five thousand natives lay lifeless on the bloodied floor of the plaza, with only Atahualpa as the sole survivor—he was left unconscious following a blow on the head. Knowing the Sapan Inka possessed more value alive than dead, Pizarro held him hostage.

Atahualpa became aware of the Spaniards' greed; he witnessed how the Spaniards looted corpses and all the holy temples. And so, in exchange for his life, Atahualpa offered them a room full of unthinkable riches. The room was more than six meters long and five meters wide, and the captured Sapan Inka promised to stack it with gold and silver to a height of over two meters. The luxurious offer was undoubtedly accepted by Pizarro, though he never intended to fulfill his end of the bargain.

Despite remaining in Spanish captivity, Atahualpa never passed his throne to anyone else. Instead, he ruled his already crumbling empire from a distance, perhaps with chains around his wrists. Pizarro, on the other hand, was never known to have stayed still for long; he sent his men out on an exploratory expedition to Cuzco while he waited behind for reinforcement to arrive from Panama. Eight months passed, and as promised, Atahualpa had the room filled with the riches of the Inca. Today, the value of the treasures would be over fifty million USD.

An illustration of the Inca people bringing in the ransom for Atahualpa's release.
https://commons.wikimedia.org/wiki/File:Oro_y_plata_del_Inca.jpg

Probably thinking he could finally gain his freedom and quietly plan a retaliation, Atahualpa patiently waited for Pizarro's decision. However, the ransom was not enough to distract the Spaniards. In the eyes of Pizarro, Atahualpa had already exhausted his role; the Inca ruler had no other use to the Spaniards apart from posing a possible danger in the future. And so, on the 26th of July 1533, the once-mighty Inca king was sentenced to death by burning at the stake. Once again and for the last time, the Spaniards demanded that the hard-headed monarch accept Christianity. In return, should he agree, they offered him an easier way out. With his life already at the end of the line, Atahualpa agreed to be baptized. Because of this, Pizarro ordered the fire extinguished. He then granted— or condemned—Atahualpa to death by strangulation while his people watched, their eyes filled with terror.

A painting depicting Atahualpa's execution.

With the death of Atahualpa, the Inca spiraled straight into a dark abyss. Despite having fewer numbers than the kingless Inca warriors, the Spaniards—fully equipped from top to toe—easily trampled their way through Cuzco, sacking the entire city while plundering every fortune it hid. They then installed a puppet king named Manco to maintain peace in the empire. This move led to a rebellion three years later, but Manco and the Inca failed to reclaim their power. Seeing no other way, the Inca were forced to retreat to Vilcabamba, a village deep in the jungle. Here, they built their last stronghold. Perhaps protected and hidden by the thick greenery, Vilcabamba remained a safe haven for the Inca for about thirty-six years.

In 1572, when the throne had already passed to Manco's son, Túpac Amaru, the Spaniards finally took action. The last king of the Inca was executed without hesitation, closing the last chapter of the Inca Empire. Vilcabamba, on the other hand, was left under the care of mother nature. Though the Inca civilization was left forgotten following their terrible fate, the accidental discovery of Machu Picchu, a glorious mountain citadel, would soon revive the history of the Inca.

Chapter 10 - The Misidentification of Machu Picchu

Some say the once mighty empire of the Incas fell faster than the fleeting moments it had taken to rise and prosper. The Spaniards had moved swiftly to dismantle the Incan society with the help of great weapons and machinery while plundering all its riches and destroying its sacred sites. Their kings were executed as if they were nothing more than the lowest slaves, and their cities were razed until each was reduced to ashes or reclaimed by the forces of nature. Vilcabamba, for one, was swallowed whole by the relentless march of time, with encroaching nature hugging close to the many structures that once stood tall in the stronghold.

Even though centuries have passed since the fall of the ancient civilization, the legend of Vilcabamba as the famed Lost City of the Incas continued to intrigue the imaginations of explorers, historians, and archaeologists. Like the Spaniards, some even believe that the Lost City holds secret treasures left by the indigenous people. Those who do not have their eyes set on the vast riches of the lost civilization, however, are more captivated by the mystery of its history. Among those thirsty for the tales of the Inca was Hiram Bingham, a man whose curiosity and passion for South American studies invited him to embark on a set of extraordinary journeys of discovery.

Born in Hawaii, Hiram Bingham was neither a trained archaeologist nor an anthropologist but an obsessed explorer, academic, and historian. However, during a particular trip to Chile, where he served as a delegate to the First Pan-American Scientific Congress, Bingham first encountered remnants of the Incan ruins. Surprisingly, this was not enough to pique his interest in searching for the forgotten city of the Incas.

In 1908, Bingham found himself near Cuzco while working on an autobiography of the South American liberator, Simón Bolívar. Here, he was persuaded by a local to visit the site of the Incan citadel, Choquequirao. After a few moments of hesitation, Bingham followed the man to the site. As soon as the man pointed to the still-intact citadel, Bingham's curiosity level heightened.

Soon, Bingham returned from his eye-opening adventures and persuaded Yale University—where he held a lectureship position at that time—to collaborate with the Peruvian authorities on an expedition to search for more Inca sites in the Cuzco region. And so, in 1911, Bingham was made captain of the team as the expedition set forth, hoping they could not only find but unveil more forgotten cities of the Incas, especially the fabled Vilcabamba.

Bingham was confident he could find the city with extra hours of work. He spent his time studying existing documents, examining both old and new maps, and holding discussions with multiple experts and scholars to gain insights into the potential location of the forgotten Inca city. This was his daily routine until it was finally time for him to depart to the remote regions of Peru.

While the opinions and theories of the scholars were important and worth noting, Bingham also understood that the most precious information about the ancient ruins could be obtained from the local farmers and indigenous communities within the Peruvian landscape. So, he engaged with these communities, hoping they could provide guidance and new insights. He was, indeed, correct about listening to the locals. With their help, Bingham and his team navigated through the rough terrain with minimal obstacles and eventually laid eyes on more hidden remnants of the Inca. As he traversed through the Andes Mountains, Bingham talked to the local farmers. Fortunately for the curious explorer, the locals were delighted to share stories of the ruins and the supposed locations of the ancient sites. All the information led Bingham from one site to another. He studied each site and marveled at every structure he stumbled on. Bingham was indeed on the right track to revive the stories of the Inca.

While exploring the Urubamba Valley, Bingham's journey took a momentous turn. Here, he met a local farmer named Melchor Arteaga, who pointed the way to a mountainous jewel tucked away among the towering peaks. After hiking through narrow inclining paths and carefully avoiding slippery stones, Bingham finally arrived at the site. He was immediately greeted by dozens of perfectly carved stone structures, terraces cascading down the mountainside, and mysterious altars within the half-destroyed walls packed with stones of varying sizes. The enigmatic aura of the forgotten city undeniably captivated the explorer and left him completely awe-struck.

Photograph of Machu Picchu taken by Hiram Bingham III in 1912 after major clearing and before reconstruction work began.
https://commons.wikimedia.org/wiki/File:Machupicchu_hb10.jpg

Bingham felt elated; he realized he had stumbled on a hidden gem that had remained concealed for many centuries (though the locals were always aware of the city's existence). Remembering the descriptions he had come across, the explorer was fairly confident he had found what other explorers could not: he had discovered the fabled Lost City of Inca, Vilcabamba. The location of the ancient city, combined with the uniquely-built stone structures and the lack of previous exploration, further cemented his thoughts. However, despite his belief, Bingham was sadly mistaken. The city perched on the mountains was not Vilcabamba but, in fact, Machu Picchu, another Incan wonder that rarely appeared in ancient written records.

Machu Picchu, which in Quechuan means "Old Mountain," earned its name from the site's amazing location on the summit of Huayna Picchu. Standing at approximately 2,720 meters above sea level, one could feast their eyes on breathtaking panoramic views of the ancient city and the surrounding mountains.

One of many things about Machu Picchu that perplexes historians and scholars is its construction process. The Inca had no access to machinery and advanced technology, so how exactly did they construct such permanent structures that survived centuries? They did not use a single metal in their sturdy structures, and no signs of mortar could be seen holding the stones together. The Incas' absolute precision, combined with the intricacy of their construction, has raised many questions about how they successfully achieved such an incredible feat.

Archaeologists claim Machu Picchu was built over ninety years. Experts debate how the Incas transported the massive stones used in the many structures of the ancient city up the steep and towering mountain. Not only do the stones weigh several tons, but the Incas likely did not use any wheels to transport them from the quarries.

One suggestion explains that to achieve such a monumental task, the Incas presumably used a system of ramps and sledges to transport the stones. Using pure human labor and durable ropes, the Inca would have hauled the stones up the mountain. It could also be plausible that they benefited from the rainy season; on the wet and slippery slopes, they could have dragged the stones up the mountain without much friction.

However, another theory proposes that the Incas were masters of a technique called "stone rolling." Using round logs, they might have rolled the stones along them to move the construction material with as little friction as possible. This method is also believed to have been extremely useful for them to move larger stones and boulders.

The remains of Machu Picchu today.

No one can live long without water, and the Incas were, of course, well aware of that. To ensure their city could be properly inhabited despite its location almost reaching the skies, the Incas installed an extensive water supply system. Once they located the nearest water source—a spring on the north slope of Huayna Picchu—the Inca worked tirelessly to build a stone canal big enough to carry twenty-six gallons of water per minute in the direction of the city. At a location where the water would land, they constructed a stairway of fountains, which still functions today.

The entire city was constructed primarily using a technique the Incas were well-versed in. Known as "Idquo ashlar," this building technique could be seen in most cities of the Incan civilization. This method requires extremely high patience and precision; the Incas meticulously carved and shaped the stones in different sizes so that, when put together, the stones would interlock, ensuring a tight fit and stability. Even without mortar, the Incas could arrange the stones so precisely that not even a blade of grass could pass through them. The Incas had also taken account of the earthquakes that occasionally shook their grounds. The arrangement of the stones was so remarkable that they would move in rhythm with the earth's merciless motion. This allowed the structures to withstand the natural disaster with little damage.

The Incas might not have a written language—they recorded information using a system of knots—but they seemed to have had their own rules for designing structures in the city. The windows of the ruins, for instance, were typically the length of a forearm, while the space between them was two forearms.

Many more mysteries persist at Machu Picchu. The more research is conducted and extensive excavations are held, professionals gain not answers but more questions. The purpose of specific structures and the circumstances of the city's abandonment, for instance, remain unknown. It is safe to assume that Machu Picchu was built around the 15th century CE when the empire was at its utmost glory. But the purpose of the city remains a topic of debate, especially when Machu Picchu barely existed in written records—even its site was relatively unknown to the outside world until Hiram Bingham decided to hike the mountain paths.

At this time, we can only rely on theories proposed by numerous scholars and historians. Some believe that Machu Picchu once served as an agricultural and trading center since the city had vast agricultural terraces in the south (the north was turned into an urban center), and remnants of storage structures could also be found around the area. Its strategic location near the ancient trade routes also provides further support to this theory.

Terraces used for farming at Machu Picchu.

Seeing the ruins of intricate and fine living quarters and enough water supply, historians can also agree that Machu Picchu was a royal city or perhaps a place of retreat for the Incan nobility. Its hidden location and breathtaking views may have made it an ideal location for nobles to escape from the demands of ruling, governing, and protecting.

Another popular hypothesis proposes that Machu Picchu was an important religious site. The ancient city was also dotted with temples, ceremonial altars, and stone carvings possibly depicting religious symbols of a spiritual aspect. Some believe it was a place of pilgrimage, while others think it was a sacred dwelling for Incan priests and spiritual leaders.

One of the several religious buildings on the complex, the Temple of the Sun, has been recognized for holding great significance in the Incas' religious beliefs. In Incan mythology, Inti was referred to as the representation of the sun. Unsurprisingly, Inti claimed to have possessed mighty life-giving powers and was once revered as the most important deity. Since the sun was perceived as the main source of energy, warmth, and fertility, Inti played a big role in sustaining the agricultural abundance and prosperity of the Incan people. Abandoning the god could invoke his wrath; without their god's blessings, it would be impossible for them to live in peace and harmony.

The remnants of the Temple of the Sun.
https://commons.wikimedia.org/wiki/File:Machupicchu_intihuatana.JPG

As such, the Inca worshipped Inti fervently. They showcased their near-perfect skills in stonemasonry by constructing a temple in the middle of the city sacred to Inti. Within the temple, they placed a stone altar. Here, the priests held many rituals, ceremonies, and sacrificial offerings aimed to please the sun god and give him the honor he deserved for showering the Inca with bountiful harvests. However, these religious ceremonies were not done at random times. Scholars have proposed that the temple also served as an observatory.

Perhaps the most prominent feature of the temple is the trapezoidal windows, which perfectly frame views of the surrounding mountains and the sacred landscape—presumably connecting the temple with the celestial realm of the gods. Using these two windows, the Incan priests would observe the sky and track the movement of the sun to align their rituals with the celestial cycles. The two windows were perfectly positioned so that, during the winter or summer solstice, the sun's rays would shine through one of the windows and land on the stone altar. This was the perfect time for sacrifices and offerings.

The Temple of the Sun also has another intriguing feature. Located right beneath the temple is an underground cave or mysterious chamber that none were permitted to enter. Known as the Royal Tomb or the Royal Mausoleum, the chamber is believed to have been the eternal home to a deceased Incan king. Since the Incas deeply revered their ancestors, preserving their rulers' bodies was vital to their spiritual beliefs. Once mummified, the body was possibly taken to the chamber to be put to a proper rest—though not a single body has ever been retrieved from the cavern. Many suspect that the mummy of Pachacuti, the Incan king who commissioned the city's construction, has been resting among mountains of gold and silver behind the Secret Door of Machu Picchu. This mysterious sealed entrance, however, has been left untouched due to the restrictions imposed by the Cuzco Ministry of Culture.

Another temple can also be found on the back slope of Huayna Picchu. Known to us today as the Great Cavern, or the Temple of the Moon, this sacred site was carved out of a shallow cave. It boasted a few trapezoidal windows, which scholars suggest were used as lookout spots, and a set of fake doors. Caves were important to the Incas: they were considered the middle world between the living and the dead. Therefore, just like the Temple of the Sun, it is completely possible the temple once served as an important sacred site where ritualistic traditions and practices were performed.

The Temple of the Sun.

Nevertheless, the theories of the real function of Machu Picchu are not mutually exclusive, as the ancient city might have served multiple purposes simultaneously. After all, the Incas were widely known for their complex and layered societal structure, so the city could have been inhabited and used for various functions.

Hiram Bingham is said to have believed he had found the legendary Lost City of the Incas until his last breath. Though his quest for Vilcabamba may not have led him to the exact destination he sought—the real Lost City of the Inca was eventually discovered in 1964, eight years after Bingham's death—his effort to unveil the buried history of the lost civilization cannot be overlooked. Despite his misidentification, his unearthing of Machu Picchu successfully brought the ancient civilization to the world's attention. Today, Machu Picchu is an icon of human ingenuity, cultural heritage, and natural beauty.

Chapter 11 - Shah Jahan, the Rise of the Man Who Built the Taj Mahal

The Mughal Empire was one of the world's most powerful empires during the early modern period. The Mughal rulers established an empire that spanned much of the Indian subcontinent, parts of modern-day Afghanistan, and parts of modern-day Pakistan.

However, just like the rest of the world, the Mughal Empire was not at all free from the tight grasp of constant war and bloodshed. In 1605, the empire welcomed its new ruler, Jahangir, to the throne. His succession was not well-received by everyone, especially Khusrau Mirza, his own flesh and blood. Leveraging on his position as the favorite prince of the former emperor and grandfather, Akbar, Khusrau rallied his supporters and launched a rebellion against Jahangir to claim the throne.

Civil war ensued between the father and son, but it did not take long for Jahangir to emerge victorious. In 1606, Khusrau was captured and imprisoned in the fort of Agra (the empire's capital at the time) following his second failed rebellion. Unfortunately, peace was never meant to stay long within the Mughal Empire as another revolt broke out sixteen years later. This time, it was spearheaded by Jahangir's beloved son, Khurram.

Jahangir's third son, Khurram, did not enjoy a close relationship with his father in his early years. He was, instead, loved by his grandfather, the Great Akbar, who eventually took him under his wing. Predicting that his grandson would soon bring his empire to prosper, Akbar and his wife Ruqaiya raised the prince in their household, treating him equally as a beloved grandson and a royal prince. As a prince expected to take the reins when the time came, Khurram was supplied with endless education, from martial arts to languages and cultural arts such as literature, poetry, and music. It was only after Akbar's death that Khurram returned to the care of his mother, Jagat Gosain. Though separated at birth, the two shared a close bond; Khurram was engulfed in terrible sadness when Gosain died in 1619.

Khurram's relationship with Jahangir, on the other hand, was complex. Despite Jahangir's recognition of his son's military and administrative skills, he was, initially, rather distant. Khurram was sent on important diplomatic missions and entrusted with the leadership of various military campaigns, but he was not at all immune to the political tensions and conflicts that took place in the Mughal court. He spent most of his time enhancing his education and training and building his own network of supporters within the Mughal court–which would be useful when the time came.

Jahangir and Khurram's relationship began to shift when Khurram began relaying important information about his half-brother. He paid no mind to the father-son feud initially but soon realized there was an opportunity for him to shine if he participated in the matter. Over time, Jahangir began to favor Khurram and unofficially named him his heir-apparent, granting him full authority over Hisar-e-Feroza, a city traditionally given to the official heir-apparent of the Mughal Empire. This newfound favor put Khurram in a comfortable position within the imperial court, as he was constantly assured that he would be the one to take over the empire once Jahangir passed. However, this all changed when Nur Jahan, Jahangir's chief consort, devised a plot to disrupt Khurram's path to the throne.

Nur Jahan was never fond of Khurram and very much preferred her son-in-law, Shahryar Mirza, whom she thought could be easily manipulated, to gain the throne. And so, when Jahangir's health began to deteriorate due to his addiction to opium and wine, Nur Jahan took the golden opportunity to begin her plot. Although Jahangir was the one sitting on the throne, he could not oversee every state matter due to his declining health. And so, the real power behind the throne was Nur Jahan. To strengthen her power, she whispered words into her husband's ears so that her near relatives and supporters would gain positions in the court.

She then sent Khurram on campaigns and missions far from the Mughal capital, hoping his reputation and influence in the court would cease. Without Khurram in court, Nur Jahan was able to carve ways for Shahryar to rise as a possible contender for the throne. However, Khurram eventually sensed his influence waning and discovered Nur Jahan's intentions. Almost immediately, the ambitious prince took matters into his own hands. He raised an army to march against his father for allowing Nur Jahan's plot to derail his chances of becoming an emperor.

And so, in 1622, Khurram led a rebellion, though it was nothing short of a failure. Just as when Khusrau attempted to show his teeth over a decade before, Jahangir defeated Khurram and dispersed the rebellion. In contrast to Khusrau, who was partially blinded and forced to watch his supporters slaughtered as a punishment (he was also later killed), Khurram was fully pardoned in 1626, though he completely lost favor with his father.

Jahangir, on the other hand, had been filling his time with travels due to the serious illness that had clung to him following his addiction. By 1627, the emperor departed to Kabul and Kashmir, hoping he could find a cure. Despite his effort to heal his sickness, his health unfortunately deteriorated. Beginning with a terrible cold, his addictions finally took a toll on what remained of his life; Jahangir passed away in the same year while traveling from Kashmir to Lahore. As he died far from home, his entrails were removed to preserve his body. He was temporarily buried in Baghsar Fort before being moved to Lahore and put to eternal rest in his own mausoleum in Shahdara Bagh. This is a location many believe held a special place in Jahangir's heart as it was a spot he frequented with his beloved wife, Nur Jahan.

The death of Jahangir undoubtedly caused another series of chaotic events to spread across the empire. The contenders for the imperial throne were actively engaged in a battle of succession. Khurram was left with no choice but to face his half-brother, Shahryar Mirza, who had managed to claim the throne with the support of Nur Jahan. Nevertheless, Shahryar only reigned for three short months as Khurram, with the help of Asaf Khan, his father-in-law, eventually emerged victorious in the feud. And so, Khurram finally realized his dream. At the beginning of 1628, Khurram was crowned the fifth emperor of the Mughal Empire, changing his name to the one more familiar to us today: Shah Jahan.

The Mughal Empire saw a path to glory the very moment Shah Jahan took the reins. Perhaps rewarding his father-in-law for his loyalty, Shah Jahan gave Asaf Khan the position of vizier. Despite her failed quest for power, Nur Jahan was not killed but was forced to live the rest of her life under house arrest in Lahore. Shah Jahan is also believed to be a ruler who valued talent. A few years earlier, the emperor had met Mahabat Khan, who, under the strict order of Jahangir, had successfully put a stop to Shah Jahan's rebellion. Valuing his exceptional commanding skills, Shah Jahan chose to bury the past and made Mahabat Khan the governor of Ajmer.

While accepted by many of his subjects, like his predecessors, Shah Jahan could not escape from rebellions held by those who opposed his reign. Shortly after the coronation, the new emperor knew he must prepare to leave his seat in the capital upon receiving news of treachery from a certain Afghan nobleman. Khan Jahan Lodi, who had a close relationship with Jahangir, had gained great importance in the Mughal court. He was made the army's commander-in-chief by Jahangir following Shah Jahan's rebellion a few years previous and held the position of the governor of Deccan when Shah Jahan claimed the throne.

Khan Jahan Lodi had already soured his relationship with Shah Jahan after failing to express his support for the emperor's succession. However, Khan Jahan crossed the line when he allowed himself to be bribed by the Sultan of Ahmednagar. In return for money, Khan Jahan handed over lands entrusted to his governorship to the sultan. This was indeed treason in the eyes of the Mughal emperor.

And so, Shah Jahan laid out his plans to arrest the traitor by announcing a promotion for Khan Jahan. He must adhere to the Mughal protocol, which was to present himself before the emperor. However, Khan Jahan immediately sensed it was a clever trap, so he fled to Ahmednagar with his family. After obtaining support from the reigning sultan, Khan Jahan confidently marched toward Mughal territory, hoping he could start an invasion. This, of course, failed terribly. When news of Shah Jahan's advancement reached the sultan of Ahmednagar, he immediately withdrew his support for Khan Jahan; the sultan was terrified that Shah Jahan might lay an attack on his realm should he continue supporting the rebels.

Despite being left with only the support of various Afghan tribes, Khan Jahan remained resolute in his determination to challenge the Mughal army. Without hesitation, he and his supporters faced their opponents head-on in a fierce battle. The rebels were said to have fought valiantly, though their efforts were ultimately in vain. They were terribly defeated, and their leaders, including Khan Jahan and his son, were executed by decapitation. In a show of power, Shah Jahan displayed their severed heads at the gate of his palace, which acted as a grim warning to those who might consider defying his rule.

With the Mughal administration in a state of order and the threat of rebellion successfully dealt with, Shah Jahan turned his attention to restructuring the empire. He understood the importance of a strong military force to pursue his ambitions of expansion and, thus, began expanding his forces. By 1648, the Mughal Empire boasted over 900,000 well-trained infantry, artillerymen, and musketeers, with an additional 185,000 sowars (mounted soldiers), commanded by Mughal princes and nobles, forming a formidable cavalry unit.

Shah Jahan not only focused on military expansion but also issued several policies aimed at curbing the rising piracy and slavery in Bengal. Through a combination of military force, incentives, conciliation, and diplomacy, Shah Jahan brought renegade tribes under Mughal rule. Several years following his coronation, Shah Jahan brought his realm to its zenith. The Mughal Empire had riches many would envy, and his subjects lived their lives safe and sound most of the time.

Shah Jahan was a ruler who excelled not only in military strategy but also in promoting the arts and culture of the Mughal Empire. His grandfather Akbar might have laid the foundation for artistic expression in the empire, but Shah Jahan brought it to soaring new heights. Even before his ascent to the throne, Shah Jahan had initiated several impressive building projects throughout the Mughal territories, including the construction of mosques, gardens, and forts. However, after he assumed the crown, his creative vision truly flourished, with many of his commissions and constructions appearing even grander and more magnificent. To this day, Shah Jahan is considered one of the greatest patrons of Mughal architecture.

However, it was an event that took place in June 1631 that led to his grandest creation. Standing strong today, the magnificent structure is known as the Taj Mahal, and it was built out of Shah Jahan's undying love for his wife, Mumtaz Mahal.

Chapter 12 - The Taj Mahal: A Symbol of Love Beyond Measure

When the Mughal Empire was at its peak, Agra served as more than the political capital. In fact, it held an even greater significance. Its strategic location along the banks of the Yamuna River allowed the great city to transform and flourish into an economic hub, attracting an array of merchants, artisans, and traders from each corner of the world. Bazaars often became the bustling hub of commerce where traders and merchants found their best customers. At the time, it was common to see the busy marketplace fully adorned with diverse goods, each specially crafted with meticulous skill by experienced artisans and craftsmen.

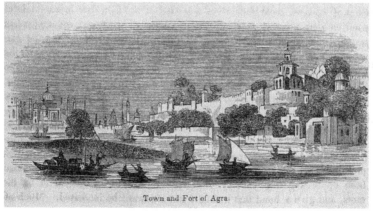

An illustration of the city of Agra.
https://commons.wikimedia.org/wiki/File:Town_and_port_at_agra.jpg

In these bazaars, a world of colors, scents, and sounds unfolded before the eyes of eager visitors. Stall after stall lined the narrow lanes, impressing passersby with their captivating displays. While shoppers were busy bantering with the merchants, hoping they could get the best deal, artisans showed off their craftsmanship by carving ornate designs on expensive wood. The air was filled with the exciting melodies of musicians playing all sorts of instruments.

However, shopping was not always why these bazaars were packed with visitors. Charity sales and fundraising events were occasionally held to support the less fortunate, provide relief during times of famine and natural disasters, or fund ambitious public infrastructure projects. Whenever these events were planned and announced, the nobles and wealthy businessmen would join hands to support the cause, either making substantial financial contributions or donating valuable items to be auctioned.

It is believed that Shah Jahan was present at one such charity sale when he was fifteen. It was not a typical event but one that would remain one of his core memories. Perhaps accompanied by his father, Jahangir, Shah Jahan strolled through the bazaar. While his father mingled with his subjects, whose hearts were eager to contribute to the noble cause, Shah Jahan was impressed by the vibrant sight of the colorful marketplace. His youthful eyes lit with curiosity as he wandered through the narrow yet beautifully adorned streets.

He visited one stall after the other, amazed by the crafts and textiles on the walls, each sporting a kaleidoscope of colors. It was only when his gaze fell on one particular individual that his feet froze. As he was standing by a stall selling beads and silk fabrics, Shah Jahan locked eyes with a girl whose presence, in his eyes, illuminated the entire bazaar—one gaze, and the future emperor had understood the true meaning of ethereal beauty. Though only a few words were exchanged, the two knew their hearts were connected and an enchanting bond was about to be formed. Shah Jahan might not have been able to spend much time wandering the bazaar, but he was glad to have at least learned the girl's name.

Arjumand Banu Begum was only fourteen when her radiance caught the attention of Shah Jahan. The daughter of Asaf Khan, a Persian noble who was also the brother of Nur Jahan (Jahangir's wife), it was no surprise her family held high regard in the Mughal court. Her best qualities—modesty and candor—were matched by her intellect and linguistic prowess.

Not only limited to Arabic, Arjumand Banu was also exceptionally fluent in Persian, allowing her to hold meaningful conversations and compose heartfelt poems—a precious talent within the Mughal Empire. Although her great virtues made her an ideal match for the sons of many noble families, Shah Jahan held the only key to her heart. Shah Jahan had captured her heart entirely, just as much as she had stolen Shah Jahan's.

And so, when Shah Jahan expressed his love for Arjumand Banu to Jahangir, the emperor almost immediately agreed to have the two young lovebirds betrothed. However, their union would not happen until five years later. In 1612, Shah Jahan and Arjumand Banu were finally married. From then on, Arjumand Banu was bestowed with the title "Mumtaz Mahal," which in Persian means "beloved ornament of the palace." Indeed, as he became emperor, Shah Jahan had a few other wives, but it was only Mumtaz Mahal whom he held most dear to his heart—the rest were possibly married due to political reasons.

Mumtaz Mahal was a devoted spouse and an extraordinary companion who stood by Shah Jahan through thick and thin. Despite her pregnancies, she never failed to express her unwavering support and loyalty, accompanying Shah Jahan on his military campaigns and administrative tours throughout the Mughal Empire. Even during moments of political turmoil, Mumtaz Mahal was always present. She even stayed by her husband's side when Shah Jahan revolted against his father. Her presence in the Mughal court was indeed significant. She embraced the roles of a trusted counselor, advisor, and confidante to Shah Jahan.

Despite the immense love and adoration Shah Jahan had for Mumtaz Mahal, she never exploited her position to claim political power solely for her own benefit. Her focus remained on supporting her husband, nurturing their family, and contributing to the well-being of the empire. Mumtaz Mahal's humility and selflessness were remarkable, and she embodied the ideals of a devoted partner and compassionate leader. It is perhaps the embodiment of these qualities that intensified the depths of Shah Jahan's despair when tragic news reached his ears.

Even though he carried the burden of an emperor, Shah Jahan was not exempt from having his own dreams. Like many others, he wished to never witness the death of his companion. However, in 1631, as Shah Jahan was on a military campaign in the Deccan Plateau, his nightmare began to turn into reality. Through messengers, the emperor was told of his wife's worsened condition: Mumtaz Mahal was about to give birth to their fourteenth child, but it seemed like she would not survive. Without hesitation, Shah Jahan rushed to be at the side of his wife. Perhaps while holding her hands, he prayed desperately that she would not die. But fate had other plans, as after nearly thirty hours of prolonged labor, Mumtaz Mahal passed away.

Some say the room went silent the moment Mumtaz Mahal breathed her last, while others claim it was filled with nothing but the emperor's wails of agony. We can never confirm his true reaction, but it is safe to assume that Mumtaz's death shattered Shah Jahan's heart into a million pieces. Ancient writers claim that his grief was so overwhelming that he fell into a deep hole of depression and mourning that lasted for years—or perhaps until the end of his life.

Humans do not have the power to meddle in matters of death; even the most powerful emperor of the Mughal Empire could not reverse the course of life and death. The most Shah Jahan could do was preserve the memory of his beloved wife. Even after death, Mumtaz Mahal deserved a grand gift for her unwavering devotion, love, and loyalty. And so, a magnificent vision took shape in the emperor's mind. Roughly seven months later, the emperor announced the construction of the Taj Mahal, a spectacular mausoleum befitting a beloved queen.

However, the Taj Mahal was not built merely as a tomb. As the patron of culture and architecture, Shah Jahan envisioned the marble structure going down in history as the world's most brilliant architectural masterpiece. And so, he gathered as many world-class architects as he could find; Ustad Ahmad Lahori was the one he was most confident could realize his vision. Not limiting the Taj to a single architectural design, Shah Jahan's team of architects concluded that to create a wonder, they must seamlessly fuse the diverse influences of Persian, Indian, and Islamic architecture into a singular, majestic structure.

The Taj Mahal.

Perhaps the most crucial step Shah Jahan oversaw before laying the foundation was the material selection. The Mughal emperor prioritized quality; hence, the architects and builders were only allowed to use the finest materials to build the magnificent mausoleum. These finest materials were sourced from the different parts of the empire and imported from lands beyond the frontiers. The white marble was brought into the empire from the city of Makrana in Rajasthan, India, while the jasper was collected from the Punjab region. Jade and sparkling crystals were sourced from China.

With the construction materials and precious gems gathered, the builders commenced their work on the Taj Mahal. On the southern bank of the Yamuna River, the first foundation of the wondrous mausoleum was carefully laid with extreme precision. Shah Jahan wished not to see a single defect in the grand mausoleum of his beloved wife. And so, it took over twenty years for the project to finally be completed, with an additional five years of constructing several other buildings and gardens at the complex.

The main gateway, Darwaza-i-Rauza.
Matthew T Rader, https://matthewtrader.com, CC BY-SA 4.0
<https://creativecommons.org/licenses/by-sa/4.0>, via Wikimedia Commons:
https://commons.wikimedia.org/wiki/File:The_main_gateway_(darwaza)_to_the_Taj_Mahal.jpg

The exterior of Taj Mahal and one of its minarets.
Matthew T Rader, https://matthewtrader.com, CC BY-SA 4.0
<https://creativecommons.org/licenses/by-sa/4.0>, via Wikimedia Commons:
https://commons.wikimedia.org/wiki/File:Taj_Mahal_Exterior_with_a_minaret.jpg

Shah Jahan was around fifty-six when the mausoleum marvelously stood before his eyes. As he took his first steps into the Darwaza-i-Rauza (the main gateway), he was immediately welcomed by the Taj's grandeur and expensive ornamentation. Adorned with uniquely designed geometric patterns and floral motifs, the gateway served as the grand entrance into the world of unparalleled beauty that lay beyond. Perhaps it was at this moment that Shah Jahan realized that his wish had eventually come true: the Taj Mahal was indeed perfect in his eyes.

Beyond the main gateway was a serene garden known as the Charbagh. The garden was divided into four symmetrical sections using water channels, which sources suggest represent the four flowing rivers of paradise in Islamic beliefs. However, the central focus of the complex is the mausoleum. One cannot help but become awe-stricken by the perfect proportions and graceful curvature of the dome crowning the marble structure sitting on its elegant squared platform. On each side of the Taj Mahal are two pairs of minarets rising about 137 feet. Interestingly, all four minarets were built with a peculiar angle: tilted slightly outwards. This was implemented as a safety measure in the event of earthquakes. Should the ground shake, the slender minarets would fall away from the main mausoleum, protecting it from potential damage.

Within the mausoleum itself was the cenotaph of Mumtaz Mahal, which had been precisely placed at the center axis of the chamber. Shah Jahan's cenotaph was added later and placed right by his wife's. Surprisingly, these two cenotaphs are actually empty. They serve only as false tombs. The remains of the two loving royals were put to rest in a sealed chamber on a lower level right underneath the false tombs.

The false tombs of Mumtaz Mahal and Shah Jahan.
Gary Todd from Xinzheng, China, CC0, via Wikimedia Commons:

The actual tombs of Mumtaz Mahal and Shah Jahan in the lower level of Taj Mahal.
The original uploader was Donelson at English Wikipedia., CC BY-SA 3.0

Regardless of the false tombs, the chamber is, indeed, extraordinary. It was meticulously adorned with exquisite carvings and ornamentations—after all, the Taj Mahal is renowned for its decorative elements. The calligraphy of the Quranic inscriptions, for instance, has been revered by many as one of the finest and most intricate forms of art. Skilled artisans and calligraphers were hired to work hand-in-hand, carving verses from the Quran onto the marble surfaces. Using the pietra dura technique, the craftsmen would inlay perfectly cut and polished gems such as jasper and jade into the marble, creating exceptionally elaborate patterns and motifs alongside the calligraphy.

Nearly every part of the Taj Mahal is symmetrical—except one. Although considered the most intricate section of the complex, the tomb chamber of Mumtaz Mahal is the only part that breaks the symmetrical design of the mausoleum. Whether this was intentional remains debatable. Legend has it that Shah Jahan never intended to have his own remains buried within the same mausoleum as his wife. Instead, he planned to construct another mausoleum similar to the Taj Mahal except for its color: appearing black and built right across from the Taj Mahal, Shah Jahan's mausoleum would have mirrored and complemented that of his late wife's. This plan, however, was probably disrupted due to his unexpected death. And so, without his own mausoleum, Shah Jahan was buried right by his wife. His cenotaph was placed slightly west of the central axis of the mausoleum, thus disrupting the structure's entire symmetry.

Many might agree that another of the Taj Mahal's remarkable features is its ever-changing colors, which depend on the time of day. At either dawn or dusk, the mausoleum appears to have hues of pink and orange. When the marble structure is met with bright rays of sunlight, the Taj Mahal gleams with a radiant white brilliance, stealing the attention of passersby and even those on the opposite side of the Yamuna River. The mausoleum's ethereal beauty is further enhanced by the reflecting pool.

Shah Jahan achieved many triumphs in his life as the emperor of the Mughal Empire, but it was his architectural contributions that are often highlighted in history books and documentaries. Following the completion of the Taj Mahal, the emperor reigned for only eighteen more years. In 1657, Shah Jahan fell ill and was left bedridden. His worsened condition led to a struggle of succession among his own flesh and blood. Eventually, one of his sons, Aurangzeb, emerged victorious in the power struggle and seized the opportunity to claim the throne.

Although Shah Jahan ended up recovering from his sickness, his son deemed him incompetent. And so, Shah Jahan was deposed and subjected to house arrest in the Agra Fort. Here, he spent the remainder of his days in seclusion; he could marvel at his beloved creation, the Taj Mahal, only from a distance. He was finally reunited with his beloved wife in 1666.

The Mughal Empire was ushered into an era of architectural wonder when Shah Jahan first wore the mantle of an emperor. His death, however, marked the end of an era; none of the structures commissioned by his successor could stand close to the Taj Mahal.

Unlike many other wonders of the ancient and new world, the Taj Mahal was never abandoned. The mausoleum remained under the guardianship of the Mughal Empire, with subsequent emperors overseeing its preservation and maintenance. It survived through the rough tests of time and continues to be remembered as a symbol of beauty and cultural heritage today.

Chapter 13 - The Rediscovery of Chichén Itzá

Central America was once a region of vast jungle and dense vegetation that hid many secrets and mysteries buried centuries ago. Before the 19th century, only a few people could say they'd explored the area, and even fewer could claim they had ventured as far as the ancient ruins of the once-thriving Maya civilization. One of the first to embark on such an adventure was John Lloyd Stephens, an American writer, attorney, and diplomat whose interest in the ancient Mesoamericans grew through his reading of early works published by the German explorer and naturalist Alexander von Humboldt. And so, when Stephens was appointed by the US president as the ambassador to Central America in 1836, he took the opportunity to explore and uncover the mysteries of the long-forgotten civilization.

With his loyal companion, the English architect and artist Frederick Catherwood, whom Stephens had met three years back, Stephens journeyed to Central America. They first landed in British Honduras (modern-day Belize), where they first laid eyes on the remnants left by the Maya: within the dense jungle was a series of ancient ruins that left them in awe. Indeed, most parts of the buildings were reclaimed by mother nature, with vines and vegetation covering them, but the intricate carvings and architecture were still visible. This was the ruins of Copán, a once-thriving city of the Maya civilization. With a payment of fifty dollars, the adventurers are said to have gained the right to draw and map the structures, allowing Catherwood to work his magic.

Copán was not the only Maya ruin the adventurers visited. From Belize, the two made their way to Mexico and Guatemala, where they stopped by Quiriguá, another intriguing ancient city of the Maya. In 1840, a year after their departure from the United States, Stephens and Catherwood arrived at yet another of the ancient ruins, Palenque. They remained on the site for almost a month, mapping and producing accurate drawings of the structures there, especially the popular Temple of the Inscriptions.

Behind every success lies great challenge. Despite having rediscovered ancient ruins, Catherwood contracted malaria during their travels. However, this did not stop them from moving on. In June 1840, the two arrived on the Yucatan Peninsula, where they explored the Maya city of Uxmal. Due to Catherwood's health condition, the adventure was cut short. The two returned to New York in July 1840. The following year, they continued their expedition to Yucatan, where they discovered over forty more ancient ruins, including history's most fascinating city, Chichén Itzá.

A photograph of Chichén Itzá in 1859–1860.
https://commons.wikimedia.org/wiki/File:Fa%C3%A7ade_principale_du_palais_des_Nonnes.jpg

The adventurers' rediscovery of the Maya civilization marked a pivotal moment in the history of the Maya. In his book, *Incidents of Travel in Central America, Chiapas and Yucatan*, Stephens recorded his travel accounts, which almost immediately brought the ancient Maya civilization to the world's attention. The ruins they found, especially those at the wondrous Chichén Itzá, opened the door for historians and archaeologists to learn more about this mysterious civilization.

The origin of the Maya civilization is still somewhat shrouded in mystery; however, historians and archaeologists generally believe that the Maya arrived in the Yucatan Peninsula around 7000 BCE. It is plausible that the Maya were originally hunter-gatherers from South America who eventually gave up their nomadic lifestyle for permanent settlements. Initially, they relied heavily on agriculture, particularly the cultivation of maize, which became one of their staple foods. These people also mastered a unique method of processing maize known as nixtamalization, which involves soaking and cooking the dried corn in an alkaline solution. This process made their diet more nutritious and less toxic. Apart from maize, the Maya also cultivated other plants, including beans and squash, to further supplement their diet.

As they developed, the Maya began trading with the neighboring Olmec civilization, which significantly influence early Maya culture. Perhaps mirroring the Olmecs, the Maya focused on constructing cities while practicing various religious rituals that would soon intrigue the rest of the world even after their fall. The Maya were indeed exceptional builders and architects. Not only did they develop their very own water purification methods, but they were also able to create complex trade networks and irrigation systems comparable to those of the modern world, all without the help of machinery and advanced technology.

Over time, the Maya civilization also developed its own hieroglyphic writing system, which possibly originated from those of earlier Mesoamerican civilizations. Compared to the Olmecs, the Mayan writing system is more intricate and sophisticated, comprising a combination of pictographs and glyphs that allowed them to record and document their history and religious practices. Impressively, close to 75 percent of their surviving writings, typically carved onto buildings and artifacts, have been deciphered today. The ability to decode these complex hieroglyphs has no doubt given us deeper insight into the colorful life of this lost civilization.

It is worth noting that the ancient Maya were extraordinary observers of the sky. Combining their fascination with the cycle of time and their knowledge of astronomy and mathematics, the Maya invented multiple calendar systems—some of which were considered almost accurate by researchers. The civil calendar, known as the Haab', comprises 365 days, separated into eighteen months of twenty days and a month of five days. In addition to the Haab', the Maya also used the Tzolk'in, a 260-day calendar believed to have been related to the movements of the zenith sun and the growing cycle of corn. While the Haab' enabled the Maya to keep track of time and seasons, the Tzolk'in helped them make important decisions, such as when to plant crops or hold religious ceremonies.

Another calendar that is more popular than the others is known as the Long Count. Often misunderstood in modern times, this particular calendar was used to measure a longer period; it was based on the number of days that had passed since a specific starting point known as the "Creation Date." The Maya believed that the mythical date of the creation of the human world was August 11, 3114 BCE. However, this particular calendar reached its cycle on December 21, 2012, a date many misinterpreted as a doomsday prophecy. In truth, the Maya never claimed the end of the cycle to be the end of the world, as it simply marked the beginning of a new cycle, just as we start a new year on January 1st.

During the Classic period (200–900 CE), the Maya civilization flourished to its peak. Their exquisite architecture was on full display; grand structures such as towering pyramids and sumptuous palaces were common sights across their various cities. Although a shared society, the Maya were never a united empire. Instead, the Maya lived in a collection of city-states, each governed by local kings. While earlier evidence suggests they were a peaceful civilization that only saw battles once in a while, recent findings have turned that view completely; researchers are certain the Maya were far from a peaceful society. Their thirst for power and control over territories often led to bloody warfare among cities. Tikal, Calakmul, and Caracol were some of the most powerful Maya cities that often waged war against one another.

Although we cannot yet confirm whether the Maya had professional soldier classes like the Aztecs, we can be sure that the military was important in their civilization. Members of the highest ruling class were selected from either the military or spiritual leaders of the respective cities, and their capture during battles was a key element of military strategy; capturing prisoners was a priority during war, especially high-ranking ones. These prisoners were often subjected to ritual humiliation at the victorious city or, worse, sacrificed.

The Maya built many cities throughout the years, with some of the biggest ones being Palenque, Tikal, Copan, and Calakmul. But the one that stands out the most and has received the utmost attention from all over the globe today is Chichén Itzá.

Chichén Itzá was once a thriving city on the northern Yucatan Peninsula densely packed with various stone structures ranging from temples to residential dwellings and commercial buildings. Established possibly in the early fifth century CE, Chichén Itzá was renowned as a significant center of political and economic activity in Maya society.

Although what remains of the grand city today are just ruins in somber hues of grey—the natural color of the stone—Chichén Itzá is believed to have been one of the most vibrant cities in the Maya realm. Traces of colors on several of the structures showed that shades of red, green, and blue were among the most common paints used by the indigenous group. Every structure in Chichén Itzá was also linked by a network of paved roadways—an impressive feat of engineering at the time, considering many European cities did not yet have paved streets connecting their many points of interest.

El Castillo, also known as the Temple of Kukulkan, is undoubtedly one of the most iconic structures ever built in Chichén Itzá. Towering in the heart of the city, this step pyramid was constructed in honor of Kukulkan, one of the most prominent deities in Maya mythology. Often depicted as a feathered serpent, the ancient god was worshipped for different reasons. He was typically associated with fertility, wisdom, wind, and agriculture. Some even believe Kukulkan had contributed to the advancement of the Maya; he is said to have bestowed on them the knowledge of writing, mathematics, astronomy, and of course, architecture.

El Castillo, or the famous Temple of Kukulkan.
Alastair Rae from London, United Kingdom, CC BY-SA 2.0
<https://creativecommons.org/licenses/by-sa/2.0>, via Wikimedia Commons:
https://commons.wikimedia.org/wiki/File:Chichen_Itza_(3326547826).jpg

Perhaps thanks to Kukulkan, the Maya were able to construct such a wonder. The El Castillo had four sides, each featuring a stairway of ninety-two steps. Including the platform at the top, the temple had 365 steps, representing the number of days in a year.

Measuring at least thirty meters tall, the outer walls appeared intricate. They were fully adorned with carved reliefs depicting serpents, warriors, and dozens of mythological scenes. As some of the world's greatest astronomers, the Maya used their expertise in constructing the temple: the location of El Castillo was not chosen without reason. Due to its precise astronomical alignment, the temple had a special visual effect. During both the spring and autumn equinoxes, the play of shadow and light on the stairway created an illusion of a serpent slithering down the pyramid, resembling a mythological scene when Kukulkan descended from the heavens.

The descent of the serpent effect demonstrated at Kukulcán during the night show with artificial lighting.

Bjørn Christian Tørrissen, CC BY-SA 3.0 <https://creativecommons.org/licenses/by-sa/3.0>, via Wikimedia Commons: https://commons.wikimedia.org/wiki/File:Chichen-Itza-Serpent-Effect.jpg

To the east of El Castillo also stands another grand temple known as the Temple of the Warriors. Due to its striking similarities to a particular temple in Tula called Tlahuizcalpantecuhtli, scholars were able to conclude that the Maya had once experienced an invasion from the Toltecs, possibly built between 800 and 1500 CE. The grand three-level pyramid was also known to some as the Temple of the Thousand Columns due to its many carved columns depicting warriors.

The Temple of the Warriors.

Spanning over forty meters wide, the temple was possibly painted in vibrant colors—small traces of colors left on what remains of the facade further support this claim. At the top of the temple, the Maya installed a reclining statue of an obscure figure known as Chac Mool. On its stone stomach is a bowl, which was probably used to hold sacrificial offerings to the gods.

Detail of the Temple of the Warriors, showing a statue of Chac Mool.

On the northern part of Chichén Itzá was another structure responsible for unveiling the beliefs and ritual practices of the Maya. Known as the Great Ball Court, this grand structure was once used by Maya society for a game called pok-ta-pok. The game was not played merely for entertainment and sports but held religious and ritualistic significance. The game was thought to be a representation of hunting and the struggle between life and death.

Measuring approximately 168 meters long and 70 meters wide, the court featured a stone hoop vertically mounted about six meters high on a wall at the center. In teams of two or four, the players had to pass a rubber ball weighing up to four kilograms through the hoop to earn a point or end the game. However, they were not allowed to use their hands or feet to throw the ball; instead, players must only use their hips, elbows, or knees, making the game harder than it looks.

The Great Ball Court.

Scholars claim that the game was played as a form of sacrifice to the gods. Often, prisoners of war were the ones forced to play the game. The losing team would then face their ultimate fate: they would be sacrificed on the altar in the name of their gods. However, that was not always the case. Pok-ta-pok was also played as entertainment, with children and women joining at times.

Perhaps the most sacred site of the city was none other than the Sacred Cenote. Also called the Sacred Well, this natural sinkhole was more than just a source of water. Measuring about sixty meters in diameter with a plunging depth of approximately thirty-five meters, the cenote was often used by the locals in their religious ceremonies. The Maya claimed the cenote as a sacred site; it was a gateway to a realm inhabited by entities higher than humankind, such as powerful deities and spirits.

The Sacred Cenote.

To display their devotion to the gods, the Maya commonly cast valuable objects, including pottery and gold, into the cenote. These offerings were thought to have the ability to please the gods; in return, the Maya would be showered with blessings and rejoice.

Precious goods, however, were not the only offerings thrown into the cenote's depths. Archaeological excavations have found the remains of over 200 individuals at the sacred sinkhole, suggesting that the Maya also offered human sacrifices to the gods residing on the other end of the cenote. Most of the time, these human sacrifices were to ensure protection for their community.

However, only one man would survive the treacherous fall into the depths of the Sacred Well. This special individual would commune with the celestial beings within the cenote and return to the ground with prophecies of his own power. When this finally happened, the Maya of Chichén Itzá must be prepared. This event would mark the start of their decline and the beginning of a series of catastrophes that would soon engulf the Maya civilization.

Chapter 14 - The Collapse of the Maya Civilization and Its Wondrous Cities

The atmosphere had just turned grim. The vibrant sounds of the villagers talking to each other and the sights of them tending to their crops were replaced with something unimaginably darker. Wooden arrows flew in the air, several passing through the flesh of the unfortunate. The clashing sound of obsidian blades was getting louder, and poisonous darts were extracting the lives of those on the ground. Dwellings burned, and corpses dotted the ground as if the city was slowly transforming into a graveyard.

This was a period of decline for the Maya society of the southern lowlands—a period that would eventually give way for Chichén Itzá to rise as the central power of the civilization. Although the exact reasons behind the downfall of the Maya are shrouded in mystery, it is widely believed that warfare played a significant role.

The Maya were warriors, so it was not a surprise when they took wars and battles to a new level. Located in modern-day Guatemala, a powerful city-state called Tikal had been engaged in a fierce struggle with its main rival, the city of Calakmul; they waged war against each other in a series of battles for slightly over two centuries. The Tikal-Calakmul Wars were considered a significant turning point for the Maya civilization.

The Tikal-Calakmul Wars were only the beginning of an end. Following the war, the Maya began to witness a shift in the balance of power, eventually leading to the decline of several Maya cities, including Tikal. Although emerging as the victor of the centuries-long conflict, Tikal was swarmed with its own challenges. At the same time, warfare continued to plague the southern lowlands, gradually shaking the stability of the civilization. This was when the Maya stopped focusing on constructing grand palaces and temples within their cities. Instead, they used all the resources they'd gathered to construct defensive walls that could encircle their entire settlement. Other less important structures were sometimes dismantled to make way for fortifications; some cities cut walls through the middle of existing temples. Even tombs remained unfinished, delaying the souls of their deceased kings from reuniting with the gods.

Apart from continuous wars, scholars claim that additional factors contributed to the decline of the Maya classic period. One of them was the recurring droughts that had terribly plagued the region. Even though the Maya were ahead of their time with water management and the clever construction of cisterns, the prolonged droughts took a significant toll on their agricultural practices.

The Maya had always been deeply religious people. And so, when natural disasters continued tormenting them for a long time, they interpreted them as signs of their gods' wrath. These wrathful gods were to be pleased, and this responsibility fell to their divine kings: Maya rulers were expected to fulfill their gods' needs at all times. And so, when the kings failed to appease their gods and bring forth the rains necessary to grow their crops, the Maya chose to turn against their kings, with some even dreaming of putting a spear to their throats. The drought-induced hardship eventually led to rebellions. As a result, more blood was spilled, including that of the divine kings.

Perhaps not content with the drought causing havoc among the Maya, their ancient gods also brought a few environmental challenges on them. Many historians argue that the lands in which the Maya settled were naturally challenging. When their cities rapidly expanded, they would require more land to house their growing populations. Because of this, they would often resort to clearing forests, which, in turn, increased soil erosion and further disrupted the delicate ecological balance. Thus, combined with endless warfare and natural disasters, the Maya gradually descended toward their darkest time.

While the Maya of the southern lowlands were on the brink of collapse, the cities in the north were enjoying the opposite fate. At this point, Chichén Itzá and Uxmal had just begun to show their first signs of great power, and they were quick to seize the opportunity presented by the decline of their southern counterparts. As for the Maya in the south, their hopes of standing on their feet again were most certainly crushed. They could no longer see their future should they remain in their once-thriving cities. So, they had no choice but to abandon their homes and migrate to the north in search of a new life. Chichén Itzá was one of the cities that experienced the arrival of these Maya. From then on, Chichén Itzá grew tremendously and quickly became the new regional power. These migrating Maya who made Chichén Itzá their new home brought a collection of new influences, skills, traditions, and knowledge. They were one of the factors that fueled the growth and development of the ancient city. Before long, Chichén Itzá flourished as a hub of activity and a center of magnificent Maya architecture.

With the city now under the spotlight of power, the Maya saw a shift in their political structure. Ever since the collapse of the southern Maya cities, the traditional model of rule by kings was put to an end. Instead of divine kings, ruling councils were established at Chichén Itzá, allowing for a more collective approach to governance. The city also established itself as a dominant force in the trade economy of the Yucatan Peninsula. Chichén Itzá thrived as a center of trade and commerce, which rewarded it with grand wealth and riches.

But, of course, its power was never meant to last; the prosperity of Chichén Itzá would eventually wane. Perhaps mirroring its southern counterparts, the reasons behind its decline vary. According to one theory, internal strife erupted within the city due to its association with foreign influences. Chichén Itzá was home to dozens of architectural wonders. But some of them displayed peculiar similarities to those of the Toltecs, an influential civilization from central Mexico. Because of this, scholars propose that Chichén Itzá was, in fact, ruled by Toltec migrants—or invaders—who had assimilated into the Maya culture. The Toltecs were once popularly known for their impressive architectural techniques. Their most renowned architectural styles include columns, warrior motifs, and images of serpents, all of which were present in many of Chichén Itzá's structures. This theory, however, remains a topic of debate among historians and archaeologists. Some believe that, at some point, Chichén Itzá was invaded by the Toltecs, who later assumed the titles of rulers; others deny the claim. Considering this theory, it could be plausible that not all Maya were content with being ruled by foreign leaders.

Regardless, one particular man, known to the Maya as Hunac Ceel, is said to have played a crucial role in shaping the city's destiny. No one can confirm why exactly he dreamed of overthrowing Chichén Itzá. He is believed to have been captured following a foiled attack on the city and was condemned to be sacrificed by being thrown into the Sacred Cenote. Surprisingly, Hunac Ceel survived the murky waters of the cenote, which impressed the Maya of Chichén Itzá. His survival was indeed thought to have been an omen of something greater. Upon getting hoisted up, Hunac Ceel told the others of his journey to the celestial realm; he claimed that upon touching the waters of the cenote, he made contact with the gods. He told them about many prophecies and things that were yet to happen, including his rise to power. Completely enthralled by the tales and prophecies, the Maya appointed Hunac Ceel as their ruler, which gave way for him to lay the foundation of a new city called Mayapan.

A panorama of the Mayapan excavations.

Hunac Ceel's brand new city, though an impressive sight in its own right, fell short of the architectural grandeur displayed in Chichén Itzá. Nevertheless, under the reign of Hunac Ceel, Mayapan eventually thrived and claimed the title of a new center of power. Hunac Ceel also gave birth to the Cocom dynasty, which ruled the Yucatan Peninsula during the post-classic period.

Although his power had been gradually increasing and his city beginning to flourish, Hunac Ceel still harbored mistrust towards the rulers of Chichén Itzá. The city was his rival at that time, and he must seek reasons to start a war.

And so, just as the gods had favored him, an opportunity to spark a conflict arose when the bride of Ah Ulil, the lord of the city Izamal, was kidnapped by Chac Xib Chac, the ruler of Chichén Itzá at the time. Without haste, Hunac Ceel seized the golden opportunity presented before him; in the name of Izamal, Hunac Ceel waged war against Chichén Itzá. In the ensuing effort, the Mayapan ruler emerged victorious.

With the rulers of the city finally dealt with, Hunac Ceel established Mayapan as the sole power of the region. Those who survived were forced to abandon Chichén Itzá and relocate to Mayapan, contributing to its growing population and development. Mayapan continued to prosper as the main power of the Yucatan Peninsula for over two centuries before being decimated in 1441 CE.

Following Mayapan's decline, the Maya were yet again on the verge of collapse—especially when a new group of foreigners violently announced their arrival on their shores. Bartholomew Columbus was among the first Europeans to make contact with the Maya. Upon being sent by his brother, Christopher Columbus, in 1502 to explore the island of Guanaja, he came across an approaching canoe that appeared to carry a wealth of trade goods from the Yucatan Peninsula. Intrigued, Bartholomew did not waste a minute before seizing control of the canoe. On board, he discovered an array of cargo ranging from cotton textiles to ceramics, flint-studded war clubs, copper bells, and a large amount of cacao. The canoe was also transporting a small group of women and children, presumably en route to be sold as slaves. Not planning to return to his brother with only a simple report, Bartholomew looted the trading canoe. The Maya captain was also captured by the Europeans to serve as an interpreter. Although the canoe was allowed to continue its course, news of the attack reached those who often traveled along the Maya trade routes.

The Maya were not renowned for hospitality, especially towards foreign faces. And so, when the Maya stumbled upon several Europeans—who had just survived a shipwreck—drifting towards their coast in 1511, they paid no mind to their explanation and immediately took them as prisoners. Some were sacrificed in the name of the Maya gods. while those who attempted to flee were made slaves for life. One exception was made for the Spaniard named Gonzalo Guerrero, who, through a showcase of military prowess, had earned a place in the Maya military ranks. He eventually assimilated the beliefs and traditions of the Maya: Guerrero not only married a Maya woman but also converted to Maya polytheism. It is believed that Guerrero stayed loyal to the Maya until the end of his life; he was among the warriors who fought against the Spaniards who invaded the Maya.

The invasion campaign against the Maya in Guatemala was led primarily by Hernán Cortés and Pedro de Alvarado. Unlike their conquest of the Incan civilization, which took only forty years to realize, their invasion of the entire Maya society proved to be far more challenging; it was undeniably a long process that lasted nearly two centuries long. By the time of their arrival, the Maya cities were actively at war with each other while certain regions were already facing smallpox, which had greatly affected their population. Leveraging these opportunities, the conquistadors asserted their dominance.

Another Spanish conquistador, Francisco de Montejo, had also set out on his campaign in the Yucatan in 1527, but his troops were decimated by the fierce warriors. Despite his loss, the conquistador established a small fort at Xaman-Ha'. The Spaniards returned to the peninsula four years later with bigger reinforcements. Planning to take the Yucatan from the north, Montejo dispatched his son, Francisco Montejo the Younger, to seize Chichén Itzá in 1532. His objective was to establish a capital on the site. Though the Spaniards successfully made camp in Chichén Itzá—the city was almost undefended, as it served only as a pilgrimage site following its decline—the Maya surrounding the area soon grew hostile. They laid siege to the Spaniards, forcing them to retreat to the ruins of the city.

With no signs of reinforcements coming to help and depleting supplies, the Spaniards were forced to put up a fight. They were obliterated by the local warriors. And so, when night came, what was left of the troops began to leave their post, abandoning their recently established town in Chichén Itzá. They eventually left the Yucatan Peninsula in 1535 but would soon return with greater strategies to take on the vicious warriors.

It was only in 1542 that the Spaniards successfully established their first important political settlement. From here, the conquistadors went on to conquer the rest of the cities dotted along the peninsula. Though the Maya actively led resistance and revolts against the headstrong invaders, the Spanish eventually emerged victorious; the conquistadors successfully incorporated all the lands once belonging to the Maya into their empire by 1697.

The Spanish colonization brought about drastic changes to Maya society. The indigenous people were subjected to forced labor on their own ancestral lands, and their resources were exploited to the maximum. They were forced to dismiss their beliefs and embrace a religion they were unfamiliar with. Should they refuse, death and punishment were always the result.

The Spanish conquest seemed poised to extinguish the vibrant flame of the Maya civilization. Their once-great cities, including that of Chichén

Itzá, might have gone through centuries of abandonment and decay. However, the resilience of the Maya culture and identity proved indomitable. They may have faced extreme oppression and defeat at the hands of the power-hungry Europeans. But even after years, their spirits refused to be silenced and forgotten. The rediscovery of Chichén Itzá and many other Maya cities following their neglect have brought them back to life. Perhaps against the wishes of the conquistadors, the Maya civilization has been put into the world's gaze. Today, the Maya legacy continues to shine brightly, illuminating the many continents of the world and captivating the hearts and minds of people from each corner of the globe.

Conclusion

Like detectives who require clues to solve their cases, historians rely heavily on evidence to embark on a journey to the past. The field of history is based on facts; it relies on the analysis and interpretation of evidence and remnants left by those before us. Without these clues, historical narratives would be nothing more than weak speculations and conjectures. With traces of the past gone from our sight, we can no longer construct a comprehensive understanding of our collective human story.

Hence, preserving the ruins that once belonged to the hundreds of generations before us plays a crucial role in the world of history. These sites could equip historians, archaeologists, and scholars with the necessary information to piece together the puzzle of bygone eras. The Seven Wonders of the World, which have been captivating the imagination of people throughout the centuries, are the main characters in this context. While these wondrous structures are often revered for their architectural grandeur and artistic brilliance, their stories often end in tragedy. More often than not, these magnificent structures never survived the cruel test of time. The ravages of human actions further eroded these wonders, leaving only stones and dust for us to discover centuries later or, in some cases, only references in ancient documents.

One such example is the Hanging Gardens of Babylon, an architectural masterpiece belonging to the list of the Seven Wonders of the Ancient World. Believed to have been built in the ancient city of Babylon, this wonder was thought to have the ability to impress everyone who passed by it. Its ascending series of tiered gardens, each filled with various species of trees, plants, and flowers, provided a grand spectacle for those close to the city. However, despite the descriptions of the gardens that have long been passed down from one generation to the next, no physical remains of the wonder have ever been discovered. This poses an obstacle for scholars to definitively confirm their existence. Without even the tiniest bit of remains as evidence, historians are left with more questions than answers. The non-existent remnants of the structure render the Hanging Gardens of Babylon an enigma; scholars are forced to rely strictly on ancient records to reconstruct its history.

The mysterious disappearance or destruction of the Hanging Gardens of Babylon highlights the importance of preserving the remnants of the past—be it those constructed in ancient times or those born into the New World. After all, these archaeological ruins and artifacts are among the few things that can connect us to our lost ancestors and shed light on their stories. These things provide valuable insights into their cultures, beliefs, technologies, and daily lives. By examining and studying these remains, archaeologists and historians can piece the puzzle of history, revealing the secrets and mysteries of the people before us.

Apart from their historical value, these wonders of the world hold other significance to our modern society. They serve as powerful educational tools, inspiring curiosity and awe in people regardless of age. They provide tangible examples of human ingenuity and creativity, fostering a sense of wonder and appreciation for our shared cultural heritage. Simply put, the wonders can act as a classroom or even a laboratory for individuals young and old to learn and explore their potential. The preservation of the wonders can also bring many benefits in terms of economics. These sites attract millions of visitors from all over the world, which eventually contribute to local economies. Through these sites, cultural exchange will also be made easier. Visitors of all ethnicities, races, and religions will learn to appreciate each other's cultures, giving way to a more interconnected and tolerant global society.

While it may be too late to save the wonders of the ancient world—except for the Great Pyramids of Giza—there is still ample time to ensure that the wonders of the new world endure the passage of time. The lessons learned from the disappearance and loss of the ancient wonders serve as a constant reminder of the importance of proactive preservation efforts for future generations.

Preserving the wonders of the new world goes beyond mere nostalgia or admiration for their exquisite facades. These monumental structures are evidence of human progress, technological advancements, and cultural diversity. Back then, preserving the ancient wonders may have been a daunting task, especially when wars often resulted in the structures' permanent damage. However, in the modern world, we have the advantage of advanced technology and an improved understanding of the value of cultural heritage. The responsibility of safeguarding these architectural treasures is without question put on our shoulders. By actively preserving these sites, we can ensure that future historians and generations have tangible evidence of our achievements and aspirations.

Here's another book by Captivating History that you might like

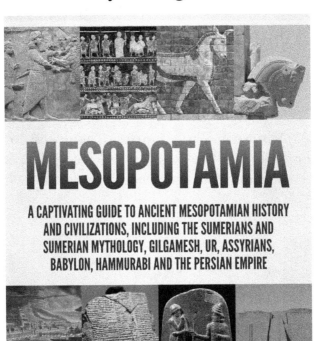

Free Bonus from Captivating History (Available for a Limited time)

Hi History Lovers!

Now you have a chance to join our exclusive history list so you can get your first history ebook for free as well as discounts and a potential to get more history books for free! Simply visit the link below to join.

Captivatinghistory.com/ebook

Also, make sure to follow us on Facebook, Twitter and Youtube by searching for Captivating History.

References

1. Ancient Greece. (n.d.). Zeus. Retrieved from https://ancient-greece.org/culture/mythology/zeus.html.

2. Art in Context. (n.d.). Statue of Zeus, Olympia. Retrieved from https://artincontext.org/zeus-statue-olympia/

3. Assmann, J. (2002). The Mind of Egypt: History and Meaning in the Time of the Pharaohs. New York: Metropolitan Books.

4. Barringer, J. (2007). What Happened to the Zeus of Olympia? The Annual of the British School at Athens, 102, 283-299. Retrieved from https://www.academia.edu/21863001/No_8_What_Happened_to_the_Zeus_of_Olympia_AHB_2007.

5. Best of Ephesus. (n.d.). Temple of Artemis. Retrieved from https://www.bestofephesus.com/temple-of-artemis.php

6. Britannica. (n.d.). Sennacherib. In Encyclopedia Britannica. Retrieved April 19, 2023, from https://www.britannica.com/biography/Sennacherib

7. Brown University. (n.d.). Greek Past: Zeus. Retrieved from https://www.brown.edu/Departments/Joukowsky_Institute/courses/greekpast/4868.html

8. Cartwright, M. (2018). "Colossus of Rhodes." Ancient History Encyclopedia. Retrieved from https://www.ancient.eu/Colossus_of_Rhodes/

9. Cartwright, M. (2018). "Hanging Gardens of Babylon." Ancient History Encyclopedia. Retrieved from https://www.ancient.eu/Hanging_Gardens_of_Babylon/

10. Cartwright, M. (2018). "Lighthouse of Alexandria." Ancient History Encyclopedia. Retrieved from https://www.ancient.eu/Lighthouse_of_Alexandria/

11. Cartwright, M. (2018). "Phidias." Ancient History Encyclopedia. https://www.ancient.eu/Phidias/

12. Cartwright, M. (2018). "Statue of Zeus at Olympia." Ancient History Encyclopedia. https://www.ancient.eu/Statue_of_Zeus_at_Olympia/

13. Cartwright, M., 2018. "Mausoleum at Halicarnassus." World History Encyclopedia. URL https://www.worldhistory.org/Mausoleum_at_Halicarnassus/ (accessed 11.1.22).

14. Cartwright, M., 2018. "Temple of Artemis at Ephesus." World History Encyclopedia. URL https://www.worldhistory.org/Temple_of_Artemis_at_Ephesus/ (accessed 11.1.22).

15. Dalley, S. (2013). The Mystery of the Hanging Garden of Babylon: An Elusive World Wonder Traced. Oxford University Press.

16. DK Find Out. (n.d.). Mausoleum of Halicarnassus. Retrieved from https://www.dkfindout.com/us/history/seven-wonders-world/mausoleum-halicarnassus/

17. Farrell, J. (n.d.). The Mother and Father of Greek Gods. University of Pennsylvania. Retrieved from http://ccat.sas.upenn.edu/~jfarrell/courses/myth/97/notes/mother father.html

18. Faulkner, R. O. (1999). *The Ancient Egyptian Pyramid Texts.* Society of Biblical Literature.

19. Foster, J. (2005). *Ancient Egypt: A Very Short Introduction.* Oxford University Press.

20. Friedman, F. D. (2002). *Egypt, Canaan, and Israel in Ancient Times.* Princeton: Princeton University Press.

21. Greek Mythology. (n.d.). Artemis. Retrieved from https://www.greekmythology.com/Olympians/Artemis/artemis.html

22. Grout, J. (n.d.). Artemis. Retrieved from https://penelope.uchicago.edu/~grout/encyclopaedia_romana/greece/paganism/artemis.html.

23. Harris, Karen. (n.d.). Temple of Artemis: Destruction, Facts, Stories, Trivia. Retrieved from https://historydaily.org/temple-of-artemis-destruction-facts-stories-trivia

24. Hawass, Z. (2010). *Giza and the Pyramids: The Definitive History*. Cairo: Supreme Council of Antiquities Press.

25. Herodotus. (n.d.). The Histories. Retrieved from https://www.gutenberg.org/files/2707/2707-h/2707-h.htm

26. History.com, 2021. "Seven Wonders of the Ancient World." HISTORY. URL https://www.history.com/topics/ancient-history/seven-wonders-of-the-ancient-world (accessed 11.1.22).

27. Hornblower, S. (1982). *Mausolus*. Oxford, England: Oxford University Press.

28. Hyginus. (1938). *Fabulae*. Leipzig, Germany: Teubner.

29. Ikram, S. and Dodson, A. (eds.) (1998). *Beyond the Horizon: Studies in Egyptian Art, Archaeology, and History in Honour of Barry J. Kemp*. Cairo: American University in Cairo Press.

30. Jarus, Owen, 2022. "7 Wonders of the Ancient World". livescience.com. URL https://www.livescience.com/seven-wonders-of-the-ancient-world (accessed 11.1.22).

31. Jarus, Owen, 2022. "Pyramids of Giza & the Sphinx." livescience.com. URL https://www.livescience.com/22621-pyramids-giza-sphinx.html (accessed 11.1.22).

32. Josephus. *Against Apion*, Book 1, Chapter 20.

33. Lehner, M. (1997) *The Complete Pyramids: Solving the Ancient Mysteries*. London: Thames and Hudson.

34. Mark, J. J., 2009. "Giza." World History Encyclopedia. URL https://www.worldhistory.org/giza/ (accessed 11.1.22).

35. Mark, J.J., n.d. "The Seven Wonders." World History Encyclopedia. URL

https://www.worldhistory.org/The_Seven_Wonders/ (accessed 11.1.22).

36. Newton, C. T. (1857). *A History of Discoveries at Halicarnassus, Morea, Carthage and Tyre.* London, England: J. Murray.

37. Pausanias. (1978). *Description of Greece.* Cambridge, MA: Harvard University Press.

38. Pliny the Elder. (1977). *Natural History.* Cambridge: Harvard University Press.

39. Plutarch. *Lives of the Noble Grecians and Romans.*

40. Rush, J. (2021, February 3). Researchers Examine 1,900-Year-Old Mummy Without Opening It. Smithsonian Magazine. Retrieved from https://www.smithsonianmag.com/smart-news/researchers-examine-1900-year-old-mummy-without-opening-it-180976561/

41. Strabo. (2010). *Geography.* Oxford, England: Oxford University Press.

42. The British Museum. (n.d.). Mausoleum of Halikarnassos. Retrieved from https://www.britishmuseum.org/collection/galleries/mausoleum-halikarnassos

43. The Collector. (n.d.). Colossus of Rhodes: Ancient Wonder. Retrieved from https://www.thecollector.com/colossus-of-rhodes-ancient-wonder/

44. The Collector. (n.d.). The Statue of Zeus at Olympia: Wonder of the Ancient World. Retrieved from https://www.thecollector.com/statue-zeus-olympia/

45. The Past Magazine. (n.d.). The Changing Faces of Olympia. Retrieved from https://the-past.com/feature/the-changing-faces-of-olympia/

46. Verner, M. (2001). *The Pyramids: The Mystery, Culture, and Science of Egypt's Great Monuments.* New York: Grove Press.

47. Vitruvius. (1960). *The Ten Books on Architecture.* Cambridge, England: Cambridge University Press.

48. Bileta, V. (2021). Roman Theatre and Amphitheatre: Spectacle in the Roman World. TheCollector.

https://www.thecollector.com/roman-theatre-amphitheatre-in-ancient-rome/

49. Briney, A. (2020). A Brief History of the Age of Exploration. ThoughtCo. https://www.thoughtco.com/age-of-exploration-1435006

50. Cartwright, M. (2023). Chichen Itza. World History Encyclopedia. https://www.worldhistory.org/Chichen_Itza/#:~:text=Chichen%20Itza%20fell%20into%20a,Mayap%C3%A1n%20became%20the%20new%20capital.

51. Cheng, L. (2017, February 14). Eight Secrets of the Taj Mahal. Smithsonian Magazine. https://www.smithsonianmag.com/travel/eight-secrets-taj-mahal-180962168/

52. Cottier, C. (2021). How the Inca Built Machu Picchu. Discover Magazine. https://www.discovermagazine.com/planet-earth/how-the-inca-built-machu-picchu

53. Del Campo, E. F. (2022, February 10). A husband's love built the Taj Mahal—but cost him an empire. National Geographic. https://www.nationalgeographic.co.uk/history-and-civilisation/2022/02/a-husbands-love-built-the-taj-mahal-but-cost-him-an-empire

54. Finelli, S. (2022). The Flooding of the Colosseum: Guide to Colosseum Naval Battles. The Roman Guy. https://theromanguy.com/italy-travel-blog/rome/colosseum/colosseum-naval-battles/

55. Great Wall Story - Meng Jiangnu. (n.d.). Top China Travel. https://www.topchinatravel.com/great-wall-of-china/meng-jiangnus-story.htm

56. Hardy, J. (2023). Inti: The Sun God of the Inca | History Cooperative. History Cooperative. https://historycooperative.org/inti/

57. Hunac Ceel. (2021). MayaIncaAztec.com. https://www.mayaincaaztec.com/kings-and-emperors/hunac-ceel

58. Jarus, O. (2013). Spartacus: History of Gladiator Revolt Leader. livescience.com. https://www.livescience.com/39730-spartacus.html

59. Khan, S. (2023). Changing Colours of Taj Mahal. Agra Taj City Tour. https://agratajcitytour.com/changing-colours-of-taj-mahal-different-shades-and-colour-of-taj-mahal/

60. Mark, J. J. (2023). Kingdom of Nabatea. World History Encyclopedia. https://www.worldhistory.org/Kingdom_of_Nabatea/

61. Riley, L. (n.d.). Christ The Redeemer. Seven Sisters Series. https://lucindariley.co.uk/seven-sisters-series/the-seven-sisters/christ-the-redeemer/

62. Roller, S. (n.d.). Petra. History Hit. https://www.historyhit.com/locations/petra/

63. The discovery of Machu Picchu. (n.d.). History Today. https://www.historytoday.com/archive/months-past/discovery-machu-picchu

64. Treaty of Tordesillas. (n.d.). National Geography. https://education.nationalgeographic.org/resource/treaty-tordesillas/

65. Whitman, M. (2022). Hiram Bingham - Discovering Machu Picchu (Complete Story). Mountain IQ. https://www.machupicchutrek.net/hiram-bingham-machu-picchu/

66. Wikipedia contributors. (2023). Maya–Toltec controversy at Chichen Itza. Wikipedia. https://en.wikipedia.org/wiki/Maya%E2%80%93Toltec_controversy_at_Chichen_Itza#Modern_day_theories

67. Wikipedia contributors. (2023). Christ the Redeemer (statue). Wikipedia. https://en.wikipedia.org/wiki/Christ_the_Redeemer_(statue)

68. Wikipedia contributors. (2023). Chichen Itza. Wikipedia. https://en.wikipedia.org/wiki/Chichen_Itza

69. Wikipedia contributors. (2023). Ustad Ahmad Lahori. Wikipedia. https://en.wikipedia.org/wiki/Ustad_Ahmad_Lahori

Printed in the USA
CPSIA information can be obtained
at www.ICGtesting.com
LVHW011921251123
764921LV00005B/29